# Profits and Prophets

Nancy Ruth Fox

# Profits and Prophets

## Market Economics and Jewish Social Ethics

palgrave
macmillan

Nancy Ruth Fox
Department of Economics
Saint Joseph's University
Philadelphia, PA, USA

ISBN 978-3-030-40555-7 ISBN 978-3-030-40556-4 (eBook)
https://doi.org/10.1007/978-3-030-40556-4



This Palgrave Pivot imprint is published by the registered company Springer Nature Switzerland AG.
The registered company address is: Gewerbestrasse 11, 6330 Cham, Switzerland

*I dedicate this book to the memory of my parents, Seymour and Helen Fox. From dramatically different perspectives, they taught my siblings and me, their children, the Jewish values of family, education, and tikkun olam. We have instilled these values in our children, with hopes that they will do the same. It wasn't until I became a parent myself that I realized how much of any success I have achieved is because of my own parents.*

# Preface

It began with a nun and continued with a rabbi.

I was trained in conventional economics, teaching and writing in those fields, until the lucky day when Sr. Francis Joseph, of blessed memory, asked me to be the respondent to the Faith-Justice Outreach Lecture on the Tenth Anniversary of *Economic Justice for All: Pastoral Letter on Catholic Social Teaching and the U.S. Economy.*

I felt up to the challenge of the economics in the document, but as a Jew, I had no knowledge of the theology, despite my many years at Saint Joseph's University, a Jesuit, Catholic institution.

I sought assistance from a theology colleague, which led to a collaboration with D. Stephen Long (now at Southern Methodist University). Steve and I taught "Profits and Prophets: Theology and Economics in Conflict?" together and began a research collaboration that concluded with *Calculated Futures: Theology, Ethics, and Economics.*

Sometime later, my friend Rabbi Martin Sandberg suggested that I look at the Jewish social justice tradition and its connection to economics and public policy issues. He invited me to be the Scholar in Residence at his synagogue in Jacksonville, Florida. That was the beginning of this project. This book is the culmination.

*Profits and Prophets* is a synthesis of economic analysis and Jewish social teaching about contemporary public policy issues. The policy issues are front page news on a daily basis. Even if someone is fully schooled in either discipline, it is unlikely that they are aware of the two different ways of analyzing a public policy issue or the conflicts or similarities between them. Both the economic and Jewish analyses are intended to be accessible to most readers. Neither an advanced degree in economics nor years of study of Talmud is required to learn from this project.

The book's ultimate focus is on public policy issues. But to truly understand the analysis, it is critical to understand the conceptual and theoretical foundations of market economics and Jewish social justice, which I present in Chaps. 1 and 2. In subsequent chapters, I analyze four public policy issues from both market economics and Jewish social justice perspectives: minimum wage, immigration, climate, and usury. The introductory chapter gives an overview of each topic.

> אֶבֶן מָאֲסוּ הַבּוֹנִים הָיְתָה לְרֹאשׁ פִּנָּה
> The stone that the builders rejected became a cornerstone.
> Psalm 118:22

Philadelphia, PA — Nancy Ruth Fox

# Acknowledgments

I have experienced many joys in this work. My scholarship has a direct relation to Saint Joseph's mission of social justice and connects my professional with my personal life.

I am grateful to so many people. I have benefitted from comments from respondents at numerous conferences, as well as an anonymous reviewer for this manuscript. My editors at Palgrave Macmillan—Elizabeth Graber, Sophia Siegler, Vinoth Kuppan, and Divya AnishSivasankaran—have provided guidance and support, which has made the process of writing this book very positive.

My students at Saint Joseph's University have helped me choose important policy issues and provided different perspectives and feedback. I appreciate the support of my colleagues at Saint Joseph's University, especially my friends in the Economics Department. Saint Joseph's University provided financial support for conferences, a summer grant, and a sabbatical leave. Hope Charney made my life so much easier by doing all of the formatting, as did Margie Aston with the proofreading.

Other individuals have had an impact. Rev. Charles Currie, S.J., of blessed memory, supported me in my discovery of being a Jew on a Catholic campus (a story of its own). My colleagues in the Faith-Justice Institute taught me the value of experiential learning through Service-Learning. I am now "ruined for life," unable to consider any policy or issue without considering the social justice implications, which enriches me as an economist. And it was no surprise that I continue to seek the advice of Lawrence J. White, my long-time mentor and friend. I still benefit from his wisdom over 40 years since my college graduation.

Rabbi Martin Sandberg inspired this book. He read the entire manuscript and served as an unofficial consultant on the Jewish Social Ethics sections. His suggestions, corrections, and additions enriched my work.

I literally could not have done this without him. Any mistakes are mine alone.

My siblings Linda Kline and Kenneth Fox, despite their teasing, have always believed in me. I know I can always count on them for anything.

Richard Langlois has always encouraged me, offering gracious help whenever I needed it. His unfailing confidence in me, especially when I wasn't so sure of myself, sustained me.

My sons, Sam and Simon, are the joys of my life. Every day they inspire and amaze me and make me proud and grateful to be their mom. Elizabeth and Carol are my cheerleaders too, providing support and advice. Baby Maggie arrived in May; our adventures together are just beginning.

Philadelphia, PA Nancy Ruth Fox

# Contents

# Introduction

*Chapter 1 Profits and Prophets* This first chapter sets the tone for the rest of the book. It is an analysis of the conceptual foundations of market economics and Jewish social justice. Both are about decision making—economics is descriptive, and Jewish social justice is prescriptive. Economics emphasizes the individual, while Jewish social justice emphasizes the community and each person's responsibility to others. There is, however, considerable practical economics in the Jewish tradition. I illustrate with *prosbul* (a work around to the remission of debts), profit ceilings and the definition of need.

For example, the Jewish tradition teaches that there is nothing wrong with earning a profit as long as it is not excessive. There is a recognition that profit must be high enough so that merchants have an incentive to produce and sell. The rabbis put a one-sixth limit on profit for necessities, like food and housing, to ensure that all can afford them.

The Talmud teaches "But for the evil desire, no man would build a house or take a wife and have children or buy and sell in business." Substitute "self-interest" for "evil desire," and it sounds a lot like the role of incentive in decision making.

*Chapter 2 What's So Good about the Market?* In this analysis of the market, I discuss the role of price, market failure, and the tradeoff between efficiency and equity, with an emphasis on both the virtues and shortcomings of the market. I assert that it is far easier to understand what the market does wrong than what it does right. It is a challenge to explain why rent control is bad economic policy and not the best way to help people get affordable housing. I analyze how price resolves the basic economic questions of what to produce, how to produce, and how to allocate goods and services. I emphasize that there is an appropriate role for government intervention in the market in instances of market failure but caution about the undesirable effects of government intervention at other times.

*Chapter 3 Minimum Wage* I begin with a historical review of the federal minimum wage and data about the level of minimum wage and coverage. The current federal minimum wage is $7.25 an hour and has not been increased in ten years. In terms of buying power, it is at its lowest level since 1968. Twenty-nine states have a minimum wage higher than the federal one. In the past few years, several major corporations, including Amazon, Target, and even Walmart, have increased the wage they pay to their lowest-paid employees to between $10 and $15 an hour.

Standard economic theory predicts that an increase in wage will lead to a decrease in the number of workers hired, but the reality is more nuanced and complex. Groundbreaking research in the early 1990s reversed earlier accepted wisdom that supported the theory. An economic analysis of the minimum wage follows with a review of the empirical research.

I then discuss the Jewish social justice perspective of people as workers and how that informs wage determination. The Jewish tradition views the worker as a human person, who should be paid sufficient amount to support a family. In fact, an employer is considered to be responsible for the welfare of workers, a direct contradiction of standard economic analysis. I conclude with a discussion of the $15 minimum wage movement.

*Chapter 4 Immigration* I begin with a historical overview and then discuss the effects of immigration on the economy in general and on native wages in particular. Standard economic theory predicts that as immigrants increase the supply of labor, equilibrium wage will decrease. But as is the case for minimum wage, it is more nuanced and complex. Among other factors, there are numerous, distinct labor markets. Most studies conclude that there is minimal effect on native wages. Most who are affected are in low-skilled jobs and do not have a high school education.

Economic research also shows that the impact of immigration changes over time. Immigrants add to federal revenues but are generally a cost at the state and local level. The last section examines Jewish teaching. Loving the stranger is a basic Jewish value; the *ger* (stranger) should be protected. The market and Jewish social justice perspectives both support a generous, pro-immigrant public policy.

*Chapter 5 Environment* I begin with a discussion of externalities and different solutions—taxes or government regulation. Externalities occur when a person's or firm's actions have unintended effects on others. In the case of negative externalities, that means that the social cost is greater than the private cost, resulting in too much production of the particular good. In a recent publication, over 3500 economists (including former Federal Reserve Board chairs and chairs of the Council of Economic Advisors) endorsed a carbon tax as the best way to deal with climate change.

Jewish teaching emphasizes avoiding harm. There is no such concept as an acceptable level of environmental damage. But there is ambiguity on this—if an action that results in harm to others, as is the case of polluting a stream, is necessary for someone's livelihood, it is permitted. But in most cases, the good of the community always takes precedence over the individual, a direct contrast to market economics.

*Chapter 6: Usury* I begin with an analysis of the determination of interest rates. I continue with a discussion of usury from a historical perspective. An analysis of the Jewish teaching on usury—no interest is permitted on loans between Jews—follows, along with the problems this poses and the solutions the rabbis developed. The chapter concludes with an evaluation of payday loans—should they be prohibited, should there be a ceiling on the interest rate that is charged, and are people better off with or without them?

Payday loans are for small amounts of money for a short time period. But a significant number of borrowers roll over those loans and end up paying a three-digit annual percentage rate (APR). They take out these loans because they have no alternative. Many states have put limits on the interest rate, and the federal government has limited the interest rate on payday loans to active military personnel to 36% APR. This ties directly into Chap. 2—are people better off with price-ceilings, paying less but having fewer goods available, or with market-determined prices, paying more with more goods available. Lower prices with more available goods is not a possibility. I conclude that the real question is why people find themselves in the situation where they need a payday loan in the first place and consider broader, structural solutions such as a higher minimum wage, paid family leave, and universal health care.

The *Conclusion* brings the concepts together, highlighting the differences in approaches, and concludes that there is a place for both market economics and Jewish social justice. I quote Rebecca Blank, Provost at the University of Wisconsin. In *Is the Market Moral?* she writes, "I am an economist and a Christian. As an economist, I believe in markets … the key question is not 'should there be a market' (and implies the answer is certainly yes) but 'what are the limits to markets as an organizing structure for economics life?" (pp. 12–13). She concludes, "there are times when other-interest is more important than self-interest, when we as a society need to respond more effectively to the human pain caused by market outcomes, and when 'freedom to choose' must give way to other values" (p. 54).

CHAPTER 1

# Profits and Prophets: Market Economics and Jewish Social Ethics

**Abstract** This chapter provides an analysis of the conceptual foundations of market economics and Jewish social justice. Both are about decision making—economics is descriptive, and Jewish social justice is prescriptive. Economics emphasizes the individual, while Jewish social justice emphasizes the community and each person's responsibility to others. There is, however, considerable practical economics in the Jewish tradition. *Prosbul* (a work around to the remission of debts), profit ceilings, and the definition of need are examples discussed in this chapter.

The Talmud teaches, "But for the evil desire, no man would build a house or take a wife and have children or buy and sell in business." Substitute "self-interest" for "evil desire," and it sounds a lot like the role of incentive in decision making.

**Keywords** Market economics • Justice • Decision making

## Introduction

One of Hillel's[1] most famous teachings illustrates an important contrast between market economics and Jewish social ethics. In *Pirke Avot, Ethics of our Fathers* (1:14) Hillel taught, "If I am not for myself, who will be for me?" The answer might be a fellow Jew because community and concern



N. R. Fox, *Profits and Prophets*,
https://doi.org/10.1007/978-3-030-40556-4_1

for others are core Jewish values. It might also be a defensive explanation of self-interest, for fear others will do the same.

The second part of that teaching says, "if I am *only* for myself, what am I?" The answer might be "homo economicus," the "economic man" described by a market economist. The rational decision maker that economists observe and study takes only his/her own well-being into account, without regard to how it affects others and without any regard for anyone else's well-being.

Essentially, both market economics and Jewish social ethics are about decision making. Economics is about how people *do* make decisions, and Jewish ethics is about how they *ought to* make decisions. Economics, a social science, is *descriptive*—it *describes* people's behavior; economists look at what is and predict outcomes. Judaism, a faith and ethical tradition, is *prescriptive*—it looks at what is and its outcomes and advises what *should be*. Jewish ethics instructs people *how* they should live.

But why do we need prescriptions, rules about *how* to live? It must be the case that people would behave differently—and presumably in an unacceptable way—without them. In this way, in fact, both economics and Jewish ethics seem to view people's natural instincts in the same way—self-interested. If not, there would be no need to provide ethical guidelines for living.

Economics is about the first-person *singular*; it's about "me." And while it may seem at times that I do take others into account when I make a decision (like volunteering, for example), I make that decision because it makes *me* feel good; that's my motivation. When asked why they volunteer at places like homeless shelters or soup kitchens, most respond it is because they "feel good" helping the less fortunate. The motivation comes from the effect of their action on themselves, not on others.

On the other hand, much of Judaism is about first-person *plural*; it is about "us," even for something as basic to Judaism as prayer. For many prayers, Jews are required to pray as a community; a minimum of ten is required for a *minyan*.[2] Although not universally so, numerous prayers are in the plural. *Baruch atah adonai, elohenu melach haolam, asher kiddshanu* … Blessed are you, Lord *our* God, ruler of the universe, who command *us* … (Rabbinical Assembly, *Sim Shalom* 1998, p. 301). Even on *Yom Kippur*, the holiest day of the year, when Jews recite the *Ashamnu* and *Al Het* prayers, the confession of sins, they too are in the plural. *We* have sinned (*ashamnu*—*we* are blameworthy; *bagadnu*—*we* have betrayed our ideals; *Al Het*—for *our* sins committed through hardness of heart and for *our* sins committed by betraying others) (Greenberg and Levine 2001, pp. 434–441).

## The Market Perspective

Most succinctly, economics is the study of how individuals and societies make decisions in the context of unlimited wants and limited resources. It is based on the premise that individuals respond to incentives and make rational decisions to maximize their own, personal, satisfaction. Firms make rational decisions to maximize their profit. The goal of an economic system is efficiency—producing as much as possible of what people want, with limited resources, at the lowest cost.

The combination of the primacy of the individual and the satisfaction of preferences necessarily precludes any judgment concerning the intrinsic merit of the goods that are produced. The market "does not regard any one individual's preferences as less worthy [or less legitimate] than anyone else's, as long as one can pay for one's own satisfactions ... [the market reduces preference] to mere matters of taste, about which it is pointless to dispute" (Anderson 1990, p. 183). The justification "because I want it" is sufficient. The possible result that Worldwide Wrestling is more profitable than opera, because of individual preferences, is of no concern to the market. As Michael Sandel puts it, "market reasoning also empties public life of moral argument. Part of the appeal of markets is that they don't pass judgment on the preferences they satisfy. ... They don't discriminate between admirable preferences and base ones" (Sandel 2012, p. 14).

Satisfying consumer preferences is desirable only if one regards the individual as the fundamental unit of society, as the market does. The efficiency of the market is consistent with the primacy of the individual and the liberty and freedom associated with it. Those who reject the individual as the fundamental unit of society will necessarily object to the market results. Those who believe that the common good, however defined, takes precedence over the wants of the individual will not endorse the market system.

Firms succeed when they satisfy consumer preferences. The market responds to consumers' wants, not their needs. Peoples' preferences "count" in the marketplace only if they have income to pay for them. This effectively eliminates those without income from the market. Insofar as it is desirable for all consumers to "count," this is a type of market failure. "[W]illingness to pay for a good does not show who values it most highly. This is because market prices reflect the ability to pay as well as the willingness to pay" (Sandel 2012, p. 31).

The market perception of the individual and the concept of the dignity of the individual are two conflicting views. One would correctly conclude that the market does not respond to or reflect individual human dignity. To do so would require a response to need rather than to want. The market, therefore, cannot directly promote a goal that incorporates notions of human dignity and an option for the poor.

The way we measure how well the economy is functioning reveals the dichotomy between market economics and Jewish economic justice, efficiency and equity, individual preference, and common good. When we measure economic well-being, we look at GDP, gross domestic product—the dollar value of goods and services a nation produces. As of July 2019, GDP in the United States was about $21 trillion.[3]

It does not matter what is produced—schools, books, guns, roads, pet rocks, or beer. Strong growth in GDP is considered desirable; slow or negative growth is cause for concern. Note the irony—if everyone gave up smoking, fewer cigarettes would be sold, employees at Philip Morris would lose their jobs, and doctors who treat lung cancer would have fewer patients. All else equal, that would tend to decrease GDP, even though most people would probably agree that we are better off when people quit smoking. Economists have taken issue with GDP as a measure of economic well-being since the 1970s. Alternatives have been proposed, but none has yet been adopted as an official measure (e.g., see Fox 2012 and Costanza et al. 2009). Most recently, Gene Sperling has proposed a measure of "economic dignity" to gauge how well the economy is doing. He argues that economic dignity should be "*the singular end goal for economic policy and basis for policy prioritization*" (Sperling, emphasis in the original). This would include affordable health care and a living wage.

One of the most significant criticisms of the market is its inability to do justice. As Alan Blinder characterizes it, "a literally free market shows no mercy" (Blinder 2018, p. 156). He continues, "If there is to be mercy, it must be imposed from the outside—which is why governments in all capitalist countries redistribute income to some extent" (Blinder 2018, p. 156). Much of the inequality in the income distribution, with a large disparity between the wealthiest and the poorest, is a result of the market. Median household income in 2017 was about $61,000, but the distribution of income was severely skewed.[4] In 2017, the highest quintile earned over half of the nation's income.[5]

The difference between CEO and average worker compensation informs this disparity. A recent study found a range of 133 to 5908 in the ratios of CEO to average employee compensation among publicly traded companies (Gelles 2018). "A Walmart employee earning the company's median salary of $19,177 would have to work more than a thousand years to earn the $22.2 million that Doug McMillon, the company's chief executive, was awarded in 2017" (Gelles 2018).

The data are more nuanced than the summary statistic reveals (e.g., executive compensation may include stock options and other perks). But even if one compares salary to salary, the numbers still show a large disparity (Gelles 2018). One would expect an executive to earn more than an average employee because executives typically are better educated and have more experience and responsibilities. To some extent, this is reflected in the market determination of wage. But is the extreme disparity explainable and justified?

That certainly depends on what causes the income inequality, as well as an individual's/society's goals and values. One of the most contentious issues is opportunity. Regardless of where a person starts out, what opportunities are available to move up into a higher income bracket? On this question, economists N. Gregory Mankiw and Joseph Stiglitz disagree strongly. "[I]n America, the chances of someone's making it to the top, or even to the middle, from a place near the bottom are lower than in the countries of old Europe or in any other advanced industrial country" (Stiglitz and Bilmes 2012). Mankiw offers a different perspective on opportunity. "[B]y contrast, the educational and career opportunities available to children of the top 1 percent are, I believe, not very different from those available to the middle class" (Mankiw 2013, p. 26).

## Jewish Social Ethics

When discussing the Jewish tradition's approach to economics, what we are really considering is how we are commanded to live our lives and why. In *Is the Market Moral: A Dialogue on Religion, Economics and Justice*, Rebecca Blank writes, "religious traditions have always had much to teach us about the moral underpinnings of economic systems and the practical rules for making an economy good and just …" (Blank, p. 1). The Jewish tradition's approach to economics does just that.

Repeatedly, Jewish texts command the Jewish community to think of others, the polar opposite of how economists believe people would naturally act. Jews are commanded to act with *chesed*, loving kindness. "For there will never cease to be needy ones in your land, which is why I command you: open your hand to the poor and needy kinsmen in your land" (Deuteronomy 15:11). "That which is hateful to you, do not [do] unto another; This is the whole Torah. The rest is commentary—[and now] go study" was Hillel's response when asked to sum up all of Judaism while standing on one foot (Philogos 2008).

"*Chesed* is an act of compassion extended without a motive of self-interest" (Schwartz, p. 64) and is certainly in direct contrast to the principles of market economics.[6] Why should Jews act compassionately? One reason is to imitate God's virtues. "[J]ust as God extends compassion to all humanity, so, too, must Jews practice *chesed* in every human interaction" (Schwartz, p. 65). Another reason is that human persons are all created *b'tzelem Elohim*, in the image of God (Genesis 1:26), which entitles all people to be treated with respect and dignity.

God created the world but did not complete it. So when people produce things, they are partners with God in the ongoing act of creation (Siegel, p. 338). People should delight in creation because it comes from God. "One who benefits from his own labor is greater than one who finds heaven" (*Berachot* 8a). But there is another dimension to creation and people's connection to God. Because God owns what he has created, it does not belong to humans to keep. Acknowledgment of God's sovereignty requires people to share their creation with others, specifically the poor and the vulnerable. To do so honors God.

While Jewish tradition requires being mindful of the plight of the less fortunate, it does not call for living simply and humbly. On the contrary, accumulation of goods is accepted. "Mainstream Judaism saw man's material welfare as a reward from Heaven, a gift from the Deity, and therefore something not intrinsically bad, but rather to be valued and prized" (Tamari 1998, p. 30). In fact, one might assert that accumulation of material goods is not only accepted but actually encouraged. *Rosh Hashanah* (Jewish New Year) greetings include a wish for a happy, healthy, and *prosperous* New Year. The prayer announcing the new month, *b'racha hahodesh*, asks God for many things in the coming month: long life, a peaceful life, and *hayim shel osher v chavod*. Grant us a life of abundance and honor.[7] This prayer seems completely consistent with the economic notion of strong greed. The distinction from market economics is that this petition to God is juxtaposed with a concern for others, with numerous commandments to care for those in need. And that word, need, is conspicuously absent from most forms of economic market analysis.

Wealth can be considered a blessing from God (Siegel, p. 337). For example, when Abraham sends his servant in search of a wife for his son Isaac, the servant said to Laban (Rebecca's brother), "The Lord has greatly blessed my master, and he has become rich: He has given him sheep and cattle, silver and gold, male and female slaves, camels and asses" (Genesis 24:35).

In fact, abundance can also be considered a reward from God, as the language in part of the *Shema* prayer, recited several times each day, indicates. "If you will earnestly listen heed the *mitzvoth* I give you this day, to love Adonai your God and to serve God with all your heart and all your soul, then I will favor your land with rain at the proper season, in autumn and in spring, and you will have an ample harvest of grain and wine and oil. I will assure abundance in your fields for your cattle. You will eat to contentment" (Deuteronomy 11:13–15).

Jewish tradition teaches that people have two competing inclinations or impulses, *yetzerim*.[8] *Yetzer harah*—the bad inclination—is what causes people to act in their own self-interest. It might be considered as the basis for the economic model of strong greed. *Yetzer hatov*, the good inclination, the spiritual and virtuous side (Ohrenstein, p. 50), is what inspires people to act with passion and loving kindness (*chesed v'rachamim*). These two inclinations are in constant conflict. *Yetzer harah*, the mundane and vicious side, gives people the drive to succeed, to compete, and to innovate. "But for the evil desire (*yetzer harah*), no man would build a house or take a wife and have children or buy and sell in business" (*Bereshit Rabbah* 9:7). When people work hard, take risks, and invent, when driven by *yetzer harah*, then more goods are produced—which is pretty much what Adam Smith had in mind with his invisible hand.

Market economics stops with *yetzer harah*; Judaism tempers *yetzer harah* with *yetzer hatov*. There is nothing wrong with profits and wealth accumulation, as long as people act with mercy and justice, looking out for the needs of the weak and vulnerable.

While there is overriding concern for the community in the Bible and other Jewish texts, and a general emphasis on "do unto others," there is quite a bit of "practical" economics there too, a recognition that the *yetzer harah* is likely to surface. It should not be surprising to find economics in the Jewish tradition. "The teaching of Judaism is the *theology of the common deed*. The Bible insists that God is *concerned with everydayness, with the trivialities of life* ... in how we manage the commonplace. The prophet's field of concern is not ... the mysteries of heaven ... but the blights of society, **the affairs of the marketplace** [my emphasis]" (Heschel, p. 102). There is considerable explicit economic analysis in Jewish texts. A discussion of three of them—the role of profit, people's responding to incentive, and how to define poverty—follows.

### *Profit*

Profit was not considered "evil" (Siegel, p. 337). The rabbis recognized that profit must be high enough so that merchants would have sufficient incentive to produce and sell (Dorff 1986, p. 35). Profit "serves as a motive for the creation of wealth" (Siegel, p. 340). There is nothing intrinsically wrong with a firm seeking profit, just not to excess. The rabbis imposed a limit of one-sixth (about 16.6%) on profit for necessities such as food and housing to ensure that all could afford the necessities of life (Dorff, p. 35). This is based on the biblical verse, "When you sell property to your neighbor, or buy any from your neighbor, you shall not wrong one another" (Leviticus. 25:14).[9] This is sufficiently high to provide enough return to the seller so that he/she has incentive to remain in business and sufficiently low as to make price affordable to the consumer. How does this profit ceiling of one-sixth apply today?

According to data from New York University Professor Aswath Damodaran, profit by industry sector (defined by the net margin[10]) ranged from –5.9% (precious metals) to 50.93% (transportation—railroads), with a sector average of 8.89%, as of January 2019.[11] Only 13 industry sectors (of about 90), most in banking and financial services and technology, earned a profit above the rabbinic ceiling of about 16.66%.[12]

In particular, in 2019, net profit margins in eight industries that might be included in goods and services the rabbis considered to be necessities did not exceed the rabbinic ceiling of 16.66% (see Table 1.1).[13] Because profit margins can be measured in various ways, the methodology and metric can significantly affect the numbers. For example, AARP reports profit margins for three major pharmaceutical companies, which certainly should be considered as producing "necessities," between 20% and 30% (Marsa, p. 12).[14]

### **Prosbul**

Every seven years is a sabbatical year in the Jewish calendar. At the end of every seventh year, debts were to be cancelled; "Every seventh year you

**Table 1.1** Net profit margins for select industries

| *Industry* | *Net margin (%)* |
|---|---|
| Drugs (Pharmaceutical) | 10.94 |
| Education | 6.81 |
| Food (Wholesale) | 2.05 |
| Health Care Products | 5.80 |
| Health Care (Support Services) | 2.46 |
| Homebuilding | 7.19 |
| Hospital/Health Care Facilities | 0.78 |
| Retail (Grocery and Food) | 2.85 |

Source: http://pages.stern.nyu.edu/~adamodar/New_Home_Page/datafile/margin.html; http://pages.stern.nyu.edu/~adamodar/New_Home_Page/datafile/margin.html

shall practice remission of debts" (Deuteronomy 15:1). Part of the purpose of remission of debts was to ensure a more even distribution of income. It applied to loans to the poor rather than commercial loans.[15] Obviously, this was a great benefit to the poor farmer or baker. But what about the perspective of the person making the loan? Would the promise of God's blessing would be sufficient for him to actually make a loan as the sabbatical year approached? Aware of the possibility that people would be reluctant to make loans close to that time for fear of not being repaid, the Bible continues, "Beware lest you harbor the base thought: 'The seventh year is approaching,' so that you are mean to your needy kinsman and give him nothing. He will cry out to the Lord against you, and you will incur guilt. Give to him readily and have no regrets when you do so, for in return the Lord your God will bless you in all your efforts and in all your undertakings" (Deuteronomy 15:9–10).

People responded by making fewer loans as the sabbatical year approached (Ohrenstein, p. 11)—that is, *they responded to incentives and acted in their own best interest.* Ironically, though not surprising to an economist, a system designed to help the less fortunate—forgiving debts—became a system that put them at a disadvantage—fewer or no loans at all. This is a perfect example of why economists are skeptical of "quick fixes" that appear to make sense on the surface. Economists search for all of the consequences, short and long terms, of public policy. On the surface, it might seem hard-hearted to oppose forgiveness of debts. But if that results in fewer or no loans, as most economists would predict, then it really is not a compassionate solution. It turns out that the rabbis were actually pretty good economists, aware that "love thy neighbor" would not necessarily overrule the tendency to act in one's own interest.

So what happened? Hillel invoked the concept of *K'vod Hatzibbur*, translated as "the dignity of the congregation." "Jewish law, faced with a valid and pressing need, has re-interpreted the law, even where it contravenes a Bibilical commandment" (Blumenthal, pp. 268–269). Hillel devised a solution called a *prosbul*, which allowed a lender to transfer the debt to the court itself and thereby empowered the court to collect the loan.[16] The court essentially had power of attorney (Novak, p. 213). This left the law technically intact but allowed for lenders to once again make credit available to the poor without taking on unwarranted risk for themselves (Dubner and Levitt). In this solution, Hillel was acting for the sake of *tikkun olam*, repairing the world (Novak, p. 213).

The Bible goes even further in addressing this kind of inequality. Every 49 years was to be a year of jubilee. "You shall proclaim release throughout the land for all of its inhabitants. It shall be a jubilee for you: each of you shall return to his holding and each of you shall return to his family" (Leviticus 25:10). Land would be returned to its original owner, and slaves would be freed.

"This is not so much a matter of redistribution, but rather one of creating level playing field for each generation, so that material advantages acquired through one generation's accumulation of wealth are not handed down" (Wilson 1997, p. 29). Scholars of the economics of poverty talk about the "cycle of poverty," how children born into poverty often end up as poor adults. The jubilee year can be considered a way to break this cycle, to make sure that every 49 years everyone starts again at the same starting line.

### *Poverty*

There are many programs in the United States designed to assist people in poverty. SNAP (Supplemental Nutritional Assistance Program, formerly and more commonly known as food stamps), Medicaid (health insurance), and subsidized housing are major examples. Eligibility for these programs is determined by a federal formula that establishes the official poverty line. In 2019, the poverty threshold for a family of four was $25,750.[17] Measures of poverty are derived from a 1963 formula that is based on three times the cost of a basic diet.[18]

Gross family income must be at or below 130% of the poverty threshold in order to be eligible for SNAP, about $34,000 for a family of four.[19] Able bodied adults without dependents must meet certain work requirements in order to receive benefits beyond the three months in three years' time limit.[20]

Religious texts repeatedly command Jews to help the needy. In the sabbatical year, fields were to lie fallow, and whatever grew naturally was to go to the public, in particular the needy (Brandow). "In the seventh year you shall let (the land) rest and lie fallow ... let the needy among your people eat of it" (Exodus 23:11).

"[Y]ou must open your hand and lend him sufficient to his needs" (Deuteronomy 15:8). "I command you: open your hand to the poor and the needy kinsman in your land" (Deuteronomy 15:11). Though there was some debate concerning whether "need" is subjective or objective,[21] need was determined to be a minimum subsistence,[22] and its determination is somewhat similar to U.S. methodology. The Mishnah established a poverty line of 200 *zuz* for a husband and wife (Shapiro, p. 55). The formula is based on how much is required to provide basic needs, much as the SNAP formula does. Two hundred *zuz* is the equivalent to about $1714 in purchasing power today, about 10% of the 2019 poverty threshold for a two-person household.[23] Anyone earning more than 200 *zuz* was required to work and was not permitted to collect the crops in the fields, because they were not considered "needy." This is a distinction from SNAP work requirements, which not only allow but require someone to work in order to be eligible for benefits. But both the Jewish and the U.S. policies depend on a definition of need based on what is necessary to a minimum standard of living based on food.

## Conclusion

Market economics and Jewish social thought view society through different lenses. Market economists do not have "fair" and "just" in their vocabularies. They are concerned with efficiency—producing the most with the scarce resources that exist, producing the biggest pie possible, realizing that some people will not have what they need. The Jewish tradition is based on compassion, justice, and righteousness. At the same time, Jews are not forbidden from accumulating goods and services nor acting in their own best interest. But these teachings are tempered by the commandments to act with mercy.

## Notes

1. Hillel was one of the greatest Jewish sages. He lived at the end of the first century BCE. For more about Hillel, see https://www.npr.org/templates/story/story.php?storyId=129706379.
2. A *minyan* is the quorum required for public worship. Ten adults (older than 13) are required. In Orthodox Judaism, only men can be counted. In Conservative, Reform, and Reconstructionist Judaism, men and women count equally, so 10 women would constitute a *minyan* on their own.
3. https://apps.bea.gov/iTable/iTable.cfm?reqid=19&step=2#reqid=19&step=2&isuri=1&1921=survey.
4. https://www.census.gov/data/tables/2018/demo/income-poverty/p60-263.html, Table 1.1.
5. https://www.census.gov/data/tables/time-series/demo/income-poverty/historical-income-households.html, Table H2.
6. See Chap. 2, "What's so Good about the Market" for a more complete analysis.
7. Rabbinical Assembly, *Sim Shalom* 1998, p. 150.
8. See Ohrenstein, pp. 49–53, for the text of the fable. The duality of human nature also appears in classical philosophy (see Plato's chariot allegory in Phaedrus, sections 246a–254e), as well as some discussion of the Christian concept of original sin (see Dionne 2018).
9. The Jewish concept is *ona'ah,* which literally means "over-reaching." For a technical discussion of *ona'ah,* see https://www.jewishvirtuallibrary.org/ona-x0027-ah.
10. Net profit margin is defined as net income divided by revenue, where net income is typically defined as (revenue—cost of goods—operating expenses—other expenses—interest—taxes).
11. http://pages.stern.nyu.edu/~adamodar/New_Home_Page/datafile/margin.html.
12. These numbers vary significantly over time by industry, while the market average is consistently under 10% since 1999. For example, in 2001, the market average was 7.60%, and industry margins ranged for a high of 34.97% (Financial Services) to a low of −51.07% (Internet). Comparable numbers in 2011 are 7.55%, 68.47% (Real Estate Investment Trusts—R.E.I.T), −1.66% (Automotive). http://pages.stern.nyu.edu/~adamodar/New_Home_Page/datafile/margin.html.
13. More recently, industrial organization economists tend not to use profit data because of their unreliability. I am grateful (as I have been for over 40 years) to Lawrence J. White for pointing this out.
14. AbbVie (29.9%), Pfizer (26.9%), Eli Lilly (22.0%), Bristol-Myers Squibb (20.9%).

15. Rabbinical Assembly, *Etz Hayim*, commentary on verse 1, p. 1077.
16. See also Rabbinical Assembly, *Etz Hayim*, commentary on verse 9, p. 1078.
17. https://aspe.hhs.gov/poverty-guidelines.
18. https:/www.census.gov/topics/income-poverty/poverty/about/history-of-the-poverty-measure.html The formula is based on the one-third of income that was required for a basic, nutritious diet in 1963. It remains basically unchanged even though that percent is significantly lower today, so the threshold is significantly too low.
19. https://eligibility.com/food-stamps.
20. https://eligibility.com/food-stamps/do-the-employment-requirements-for-eligibility-apply-to-everyone Legislative efforts to toughen the work requirements were not successful in 2018. The Department of Agriculture is proposing regulatory changes to increase work requirements https://www.npr.org/2018/12/20/678593200/sidestepping-congress-trump-administration-proposes-more-work-rules-for-food-sta). https://www.npr.org/2018/12/20/678593200/sidestepping-congress-trump-administration-proposes-more-work-rules-for-food-sta).
21. See Ohrenstein, pp. 164–167 and Sherwin, pp. 87–88, for a discussion of need as subjective and individual so that someone from a "good family" who becomes poor needs more than a person who was always poor. "If a person (who was rich) has become poor and requires public assistance, if he had been used to vessels of gold (to eat and drink from), then give him vessels of gold; if of silver, then give him vessels of silver."
22. This is based on the verse "you are required to maintain him but not to enrich him" (Keth. 67b). See Ohrenstein, p. 167.
23. https://eligibility.com/food-stamps Shapiro makes this calculation based on how much bread 200 zuz would buy and the price of bread in 1983 and calculates an equivalent of $666 in 1983 dollars. I adjusted that for inflation since 1983 for the 2019 equivalent using https://www.dollartimes.com/inflation/inflation.php?amount=10000&year=1983. See Shapiro, especially p. 56, for a description of his methodology.

## Bibliography

Anderson, Elizabeth. "The Ethical Limitations of the Market." *Economics and Philosophy*, 6(2), October 1990, pp. 179–205.

Blank, Rebecca M. and William McGurn. *Is the Market Moral? A Dialogue on Religion, Economics and Justice*. Washington, DC: The Brookings Institution, 2004.

Blinder, Alan S. *Advice and Dissent: Why America Suffers When Economics and Politics Collide*. Basic Books, 2018.

Blumenthal, Aaron H. "An Aliyah for Women." *Conservative Judaism and Jewish Law,* Seymour Siegel and Elliot Gertel editors. New York: The Rabbinical Assembly, 1977, pp. 266–280.

Brandow, Jonathan. "There's Gleaning to Do: How Ancient Sabbatical Laws can work in a Modern Economy." *Tablet*, October 6, 2014. https://www.tabletmag.com/jewish-life-and-religion/185127/shmita-modern-economy

Costanza, Robert, Maureen Hart, Stephen Posner, and John Talberth. "Beyond GDP: The Need for New Measures of Progress." *The Pardee Papers*/No.4/ January 2009. https://www.bu.edu/pardee/files/documents/PP-004-GDP.pdf

Dionne, E.J. "The Virtue of original sin liberalism." *Philadelphia Inquirer*. April 1, 2018. http://www.philly.com/philly/opinion/commentary/the-virtue-of-original-sin-liberalism-opinion-20180402.html

Dorff, Elliot N. "Jewish Perspectives on the Poor" in *The Poor Among Us: Jewish Tradition and Social Policy*. American Jewish Committee, 1986

Fox, Justin. "The Economics of Well-Being." *Harvard Business Review*. January-February, 2012. https://hbr.org/2012/01/the-economics-of-well-being

Gelles, David. "Want to Make Money Like a C.E.O.? Work for 275 Years." *The New York Times*. May 25, 2018. https://www.nytimes.com/2018/05/25/business/highest-paid-ceos-2017.html?module=inline

Greenberg, Rabbi Sidney and Rabbi Jonathan D. Levine (editors). *The New Mahzor for Rosh Hashanah and Yom Kippur*. The Prayer Book Press of Media Judaica, Inc., 2001

Heschel, Abraham Joshua. *The Insecurity of Freedom: Essays on Human Existence*. New York: Farrar Straus & Giroux, 1966.

Jewish Virtual Library. "Ona'ah." https://www.jewishvirtuallibrary.org/ona-x0027-ah

Mankiw, N. Gregory. "Defending the One Percent." *Journal of Economic Perspectives*. Vol 27, Number 3, Summer 2013, pp. 21–34. https://www.aeaweb.org/articles?id=10.1257/jep.27.3.21

Marsa, Linda. "A 5-Point Plan to Lower $R_X$ Prices." AARP.ORG/*Bulletin*, May 2019, pp. 9–16.

Novak, David. Jewish Social Ethics. New York: Oxford University Press 1992.

NYU. http://pages.stern.nyu.edu/~adamodar/New_Home_Page/datafile/margin.html

Philogos. "The Rest is Commentary." *Forward*, September 24, 2008. https://forward.com/culture/14250/the-rest-of-of-the-rest-is-commentary-02564/

The Rabbinical Assembly. *Etz Hayim: Torah and Commentary*. Jewish Publication Society, 2001.

The Rabbinical Assembly. *Siddur Sim Shalom for Shabbat and Festivals*. New York, NY: The United Synagogue of Conservative Judaism, 1998.

Sandel, Michael J. *What Money Can't Buy: The Moral Limits of Markets.* Farrar, Straus and Giroux, 2012.

Schwartz, Rabbi Sidney. *Judaism and Justice: The Jewish Passion to Repair the World.* Woodstock, Vermont: Jewish Lights Publishing, 2006.

Shapiro, Aharon. "The Treatment of Poverty in the Talmud." *International Review of Economics and Ethics.* Vol. 1, no. 2, p. 56 1986.

Sherwin, Byron L. "The U.S. Catholic Bishops' Pastoral Letter on the Economy and Jewish Tradition" Chapter 7 in *Prophetic Visions and Economic Realities: Protestants, Jews & Catholics Confront the Bishops' Letter on the Economy*, Charles R. Strain, editor. Grand Rapids, Michigan: William B. Eerdmans Publishing Company, 1989, pp 81–92.

Siegel, Seymour. "A Jewish View of Economic Justice." *Contemporary Jewish Ethics and Morality*, Elliot N. Dorff and Louis E Newman, editors. New York: Oxford University Press, 1995, pp. 336–343.

Sperling, Gene. "Economic Dignity: We must not lose sight of what economic policy is all about: allowing people to lead dignified lives." *Democracy: A Journal of Ideas.* Spring 2019, No. 52.

Stiglitz, Joseph E. and Linda J. Bilmes. "The 1 Percent's Problem." *Vanity Fair.* May 31, 2012. https://www.vanityfair.com/news/2012/05/joseph-stiglitz-the-price-on-inequality

Tamari, Meir. *With All Your Possessions: Jewish Ethics and Economic Life.* Northvale, New Jersey: Jason Aronson, Inc., 1998.

Wilson, Rodney. *Economics, Ethics and Religion.* New York, NY: New York University Press, 1997.

Yuhas, Alan. "Cyclone Idai May Be 'One of the Worst' Disasters in the Southern Hemisphere." *The New York Times*, March 19, 2019. https://www.nytimes.com/2019/03/19/world/africa/cyclone-idai-mozambique.html

CHAPTER 2

# What's So Good About the Market?

**Abstract** This chapter is an introduction to market economics—the role of price, market failure, and the trade-off between efficiency and equity, with an emphasis on both the virtues and shortcomings of the market. I assert that it is far easier to understand what the market does wrong than what it does right. Price resolves the basic economic questions of what to produce, how to produce, and how to allocate goods and services. There is an appropriate role for government intervention in the market in instances of market failure, but there may be undesirable effects of government intervention at other times.

**Keywords** Trade-off • Government • Market • Price

## Introduction

In a world of poverty, injustice, and inequality, it is easy to condemn the market. It is far more difficult to understand and to appreciate the virtues of the market system. There are several possible reasons why this is so. Very little technical expertise is required to observe what the market does not do, or what the market does poorly, while a more sophisticated understanding of economic theory is required to appreciate the virtues of the market. Some are uncomfortable with the basic premises of the market, even when it functions perfectly. There is often misunderstanding about what market is able to do and what it is not able to do. Under some



N. R. Fox, *Profits and Prophets*,
https://doi.org/10.1007/978-3-030-40556-4_2

conditions, the market cannot function efficiently, and government intervention is required. And there are some things that the market, even under ideal conditions, is unable to accomplish. Any valid criticism of the market must first distinguish among these. In this chapter, I will offer both a defense of the market and an analysis of its shortcomings.

## How a Market Works and the Role of Price

"A market system is a form of economic organization in which resource allocation decisions are left to individual producers and consumers acting in their own best interest without central direction" (Baumol and Blinder, p. 50). As any introductory economics student will explain, an economic system must answer three questions: (1) What to produce? (2) How to produce? and (3) How to allocate what has been produced? A free market system answers these questions in the following way: (1) produce the goods and services that the consumers want, (2) produce those goods and services in the lowest cost manner, and (3) distribute the goods and services to the individuals who want them the most strongly. The one-word explanation as to how the market accomplishes all this is *price*, which serves three primary functions in the market: (1) it provides information; (2) it creates incentives to produce at minimum cost; and (3) it distributes income (Friedman and Friedman, p. 14).

There are two basic premises regarding how economic actors behave: individuals maximize and respond to incentives. The market consists of demanders and suppliers; consumers demand goods and services, and producers supply them.[1]

Consumers maximize utility, roughly defined as satisfaction. Utility depends on an individual's preferences: movie lovers' utility increases as they view more movies; ice cream lovers' as they eat more Haagen Dazs. Regardless of particular preferences, consumers respond to the Law of Diminishing Marginal Utility. Diminishing marginal utility tells us that as consumption increases, utility increases at a decreasing rate; the utility of consuming the third slice of pizza is less than the utility of the second. Therefore, consumers are willing to pay less for each successive slice. This law translates into a downward sloping demand curve—as price increases, quantity demanded decreases. When the price of candy bars is $1, we expect people with a sweet tooth to demand more candy than when the price is $2.

Firms maximize profit, the difference between revenue and cost. Costs include both costs of production, such as labor, raw materials, utilities, interest payments, as well as opportunity cost, the value of the firm's next best alternative. If costs are held constant, profits increase as price increases, which translates into an upward sloping supply curve—as price increases, quantity supplied increases. When the price of candy bars is $2, we expect firms to supply more candy than when the price is $1.

Friedman uses the example of the production of pencils to illustrate the role of price as an incentive to produce in the lowest cost way. "Suppose one kind of wood becomes scarcer and therefore more expensive than another. The pencil manufacturer gets that information through a rise in the price of the first kind of wood. Because his income, too, is determined by the difference between sales receipts and costs, he has an incentive to economize on that [more expensive] kind of wood" (Friedman and Friedman, pp. 18–19).

It may seem logical that low prices are good for consumers, and high prices are good for producers, and vice versa. But it is not necessarily true, because that is only one part of a more complex process.

Given the choice of paying $50 for a pair of shoes or $70 for that same pair of shoes, any rational consumer will choose the former. Similarly, any producer would prefer to sell a pair of shoes for $70 instead of selling that same pair of shoes for $50. But neither of these alternatives offers realistic options.

Begin with an equilibrium price of $70 for these shoes. What happens when the price is lowered to $50 independent of the signals of the market? The shoe producer is no longer earning an adequate profit on the shoes and will not produce as many as when the price was $70. Consumers who are willing to buy shoes at a price of $50 (more than the number of consumers than when the price was $70) find that there are not enough shoes to be bought. The right question is not "does the consumer prefer to buy shoes at a price of $50 or $70?" Instead, the correct question is whether the consumer prefers to buy fewer shoes at a price of $50 or more shoes at a price of $70. Similarly, it is inaccurate to ask whether the producer prefers to sell shoes at $70 or $50. The producer will be able to sell more shoes at $50 than at $70, so the correct question is whether the producer prefers to sell more shoes at $50 or fewer shoes at $70.

How does price convey information? Suppose an e-coli scare decreases the demand for a lettuce, which decreases the equilibrium price. Lettuce growers will respond to the decrease in price by supplying less lettuce, a good thing for society if the e-coli causes it to be a health risk. Do the firms need to know that it was the e-coli scare that caused the equilibrium price to decline? Would they react any differently if they did? The answer to both questions is no. This example illustrates one of the ways in which the market transmits information at minimal cost; it makes only the necessary information available to the economic actors who need to know.

The market rewards individual selfishness. At first, this may appear to be something negative, especially because in rewarding selfishness the market encourages this type of putatively undesirable behavior. Therefore, it is necessary to understand how the market rewards selfishness and the consequences for society of such rewards. One person's selfish behavior is rewarded in so far as he/she satisfies the wants of another.[2] Is it taking advantage of someone to offer him/her what he/she wants for the price he/she is willing to pay? A free market advocate would respond that such behavior is desirable; the better one meets the wants of another, the higher is his reward (Gordon and Schearmur, p. 42). In the context of free market exchange, taking advantage, certainly a term with negative connotations, instead means to "respond to another's demand. Benefiting oneself by providing what others want is the *raison d'être* of the market" (Gordon and Schearmur, p. 44).

In a market economy, both sides to a transaction benefit, each acting to further its own best interests. Both sides enter into the transaction voluntarily; no force or outside authority is necessary to complete the trade. The commonly held belief that one party is taking advantage of the other by charging a price for a good or service someone wants and is willing to pay for is therefore rendered false. This conclusion follows from the fact that both economic agents are engaging in voluntary behavior. In a market transaction, no one benefits at the expense of the other, because if either party did not consider himself/herself better off as a result of the economic transaction, he/she would not enter into it in the first place.[3]

The signals and rewards of the market lead a self-interested person to wake up in the morning and produce not what he wants, but what others want. "Not in the quantities he prefers, but in the quantities his neighbors prefer. Not at the price he dreams of charging, but at a price reflecting how much his neighbors value what he has done" (Buchholz, pp. 21–22). The market automatically causes "self-interested Johns to satisfy strangers. No central planner need call, no taskmaster need coerce" (Buchholz, p. 24). What other incentive could function as well as a reward for effort? "[Something] unreliable, like altruism; some[thing] perilous, like collective loyalty, some[thing] intolerable, like coercion or oppression?" (Okun, p. 119). None of these alternatives will work as well as price, either because they are not consistently part of human nature or because they are not voluntary.

The substitute of a central planner, in most cases some form of government, cannot accomplish what the market can. Central planners make decisions according to one of three criteria: "according to their own preferences, their idea of what is right for society, or their perceptions of the preferences of the population" (Schotter, p. 43). All of these alternatives contradict the notion of the individual as the fundamental unit of society, usurping the sovereignty of the consumer. The last alternative is clearly inefficient because no one is more knowledgeable about his/her own preferences than the individual himself/herself. Nothing can elicit necessary information as efficiently as the price system.

Self-interest is more powerful than altruism. Such help often comes in the form of small gestures over a finite period of time in which specific need can be identified, which the philosopher David Hume calls "limited altruism" (Buchanan, p. 18). Although there are certainly instances where people respond generously to the needs of strangers, as in donations in time of natural disasters, for most people, such help is limited in duration.

For example, there were over 30 natural disasters in the United States in 2017 and 2018, causing over $1 billion in damage (Bergdoll et al. 2019). A University of Indiana study found that "Approximately 30 percent of U.S. households made a disaster-related donation in 2017 (31 percent) and in 2018 (29 percent)." But in 2018, "(only) about 5 percent of U.S. households donated to provide continued support for disasters that occurred in 2017, and another nearly 3 percent donated to support aid efforts for disasters that occurred prior to 2017" (Bergdoll et al. 2019).

The April 15, 2019 fire that destroyed parts of Notre Dame Cathedral provides another example. Only four months after the fire, donors had pledged about $950 million, much within days of the fire (Walt 2019, p. 37).

"[T]he irony is not lost on Notre Dame's staff and supporters, who for years had struggle to raise money for even urgent repairs" (Walt 2019, p. 37). For two years before fire, they raised only $4 million, "including a four-year restoration of the now destroyed spire" (Walt 2019, p. 37). Some believe that if they had been able to raise more funds and make needed repairs, the damage from the fire would not have been so severe (Walt 2019, p. 37).

Consider too that real expenditures, at times considerable, are required to attract people to participate in these efforts. There is a cost to communicating a particular problem, raising the money or needed goods, and distributing them. Among the largest U.S. charities, the average cost of raising $1 was 11 cents (Barrett).

When people act out of true feelings of altruism, they experience nothing in return for their good deeds. Studies have shown that although some are motivated to give out of pure altruism, others give to obtain tax benefits or to enhance their social status (Faculty). The term "warm-glow giving" describes this type of motivation to donate or help in other ways. These include "social pressure, sympathy, guilt, or the desire to earn prestige and respect" (Fernandez).

Some consider altruism to be like any other commodity in the sense that it is scarce and can be used up. "[M]oral sentiments (such as altruism or civic duty) are scarce resources that are depleted with use. Markets, which rely on self-interest, spare us from using up the limited supply of virtue" (Sandel, p. 126).[4]

The market is the most effective way to collect and disseminate information necessary for decision making in the market. "The competitive market is an extremely efficient information procession device that allows individually scattered bits of local information known only to specialists to be exchanged at minimal cost in order to coordinate social activity efficiently" (Schotter, p. 41).

Price serves as the signal to both producers and consumers. Price attracts resources to the production of goods that consumers demand. Consider this example:

Suppose I produce the most delicious tomato soup, with $5 worth of fresh, organic tomatoes in each batch. I set a price of $10 per serving, but no one is willing to buy them, and I go out of business. Apparently, no one thinks this soup is worth $10. And the invisible hand applauds—why?

I am charging too much for a good nobody wants and using up a resource, the organic tomatoes, that could have been used to produce something that consumers do want. If instead, I use the tomatoes to make organic pizza sauce and charge $10 a serving, I can earn $5 profit a batch. If I raise the price, I would likely lose customers to rivals charging less. If there are no rivals, then it is likely that firms will enter this profitable business, which will bring down the price.[5]

The strength of the market as a mechanism for disseminating information in the most efficient manner has its foundation in the individual as the basic unit of society. "An individual is the world's foremost expert on what she wants. Nobody knows better; nobody else can better judge the effects of alternative choices on her achieving what she wants. Therefore, people should look after their own interests. If all sought to do the 'public good,' they would have to know as much about everyone else as themselves" (Buchholz, p. 30).

What keeps consumers from offering too low a price and producers from selling at too high a price? A consumer who is willing and able to pay $1 for a candy bar may find that producers are not willing to supply sufficient candy bars at that price. There is an incentive for consumers to offer a higher price. What keeps producers from selling at too high a price? Similar logic indicates that some producers who are willing to sell candy at $2 may not be able to find a buyer at that price; they are left with unsold candy. There is an incentive for producers to sell at a lower price. Eventually, the price at which producers are willing to sell equals the price at which consumers are willing to buy—the equilibrium price. At the equilibrium price, say $1.50, all consumers who are willing and able to buy candy at $1.50 can do so, and all producers who are willing to sell candy at $1.50 can do so. There is no incentive for either the buyer or the seller to change behavior.

Notice the language—all consumers who are willing to pay $1.50 for a candy bar can. Some consumers do not feel that a candy bar is worth $1.50; accordingly, these consumers will not purchase a candy bar at a price of $1.50.

At a price of $1.50, there may be some consumers who are *unable* to buy a candy bar, most likely because of inadequate income. The language of market analysis that the market satisfies consumers' *wants*, as opposed to their *needs*, is crucial. The mechanism of equilibrium, via price, does not guarantee that everyone gets what they need. In the case of the candy bars, there is not much of a problem. But if the example were insulin or a winter coat or heating fuel, many would decry the market as unfair and demand a non-market solution. The proposed solution often comes in the form of price controls—a mandated price below equilibrium that is considered fair and that will allow all who need the good to be able to buy it.

But decreasing price is not necessarily good for the consumers who cannot afford the good at the equilibrium price. As price is lowered below equilibrium by fiat, say to $1.25, two things happen. Consumers will demand more candy bars (the Law of Demand), and producers will supply fewer. At the fairer, below equilibrium price, some consumers who are willing to buy candy bars at $1.25 will be unable to do so, because at a price of $1.25, fewer candy bars are for sale. When price is lowered to $1.25, *independent of the signals of the market*, the candy bar producer is no longer earning an adequate profit on candy bars and will not produce as many as when the price was $1.50. More candy bars cannot be bought because more are not being produced.

Sellers are sometimes accused of price gouging when they increase prices in the wake of increased demand that follows natural disasters. Take the example of recent wildfires in California, which destroys countless homes. After the fires, the demand for building materials increases because people want to rebuild their homes. In response to this increased demand, the price of building materials increases. Suppliers are accused of cruelly price gouging, an unethical practice that inflicts further pain and suffering on those already affected by the fires. How could an economist argue that these price increases benefit society?

The increase in price is a signal to those who are interested—in this case the consumers wishing to reconstruct their homes and the builders who are selling the materials—that the building materials are scarcer and hence more valuable than they were before the fires. As the price increases, those homeowners who might have otherwise purchased these materials to make a minor repair, such as a crack in a patio, are likely to postpone the purchase until the prices decline, which frees up that material to those who want it more, to reconstruct homes that were actually destroyed. As the price increases, suppliers of the material have an incentive to bring more supplies to market—not because of altruistic feelings for those who are homeless, but because they stand to make a profit.

There are not enough building materials supplied at the pre-fire price to satisfy the increase in demand. At the higher price, all consumers who are willing and able to make a purchase at that price can. It is beneficial to society for the marginal consumers, those with less desperate desire, to cut back on consumption and for suppliers to bring more building materials to market—an increase in price accomplishes both of these things. If, out of a feeling of justice, the government had mandated that the prices of building materials remained at the pre-fire level, neither of these results could or would have occurred. There would still have been a shortage of building materials. Lowering the price does not solve the problem of excess demand; no more goods are available as a result.[6]

Under price controls, an alternative method of allocating the scarce resource must be found. These may include rationing, first come first served, or a black market. When price is not determined in the market, such as when there is ticket scalping, the rewards may be earned by a third party and not the producer. N. Gregory Mankiw describes this phenomenon in his article about purchasing tickets for *Hamilton* for $2500 each (Mankiw).

In its role as distributor of income, price creates an entire class of people who do not have the very basics in human necessities of food, shelter, education, and medical care. Those who produce goods and services most highly valued in the economy are the most richly compensated; in the market, that compensation is determined independent of need. The function of allocation of income cannot be separated from price. "If what a person gets does not depend on the price he receives for the services of his resources, what incentive does he have to seek out information on prices or to act on the basis of that information? If prices are prevented from affecting the distribution of income, they cannot be used for other purposes" (Friedman and Friedman, p. 23).

## What Is Wrong with the Market?

If the market works so wondrously, why would anyone, even economists, criticize it? Shortcomings of the market typically fall into one of three categories: market failure, disagreement with the basic premises, and social justice.

The market achieves an efficient outcome only when certain conditions are satisfied. When they are not, a situation of market failure results, and government intervention is required to achieve an efficient outcome. Externalities, public good, and market power are the primary causes of market failure. Only externalities have a direct application to policy issues discussed in later chapters. A brief discussion of public goods and market power can be found in the Appendix to this chapter. Even when the market outcome is efficient, some basic premises of the model may be questioned. Finally, an efficient market outcome is not just.

### *Externalities*

Externalities are sometimes known as unintended, or spillover, effects. When an individual decision maker does not incur all of the costs or benefits of his/her decision, the result is inefficient. Pollution is a common example of a negative externality. A paper firm pays for the inputs used in the production of its final product and includes these costs of production in its determination of the profit maximizing level of output. It also produces air pollution, which has negative health effects on local inhabitants. The paper firm does not pay for these negative effects, and it therefore produces more pollution (a by-product of its paper production) than is efficient.[7]

There are two basic alternatives to correct the problem. The government can adjust the market so that the firm incurs the cost of pollution; this policy is known as internalizing the externality. Such policy is usually accomplished via taxes, which raise the cost of paper production, causing a profit maximizing (cost minimizing) firm to decrease production of its output and concurrently decrease pollution. An alternative and more common policy is for the government to mandate the desired level of pollution and to impose fines if the firm does not comply. Banning smoking or single-use plastic bags are examples. In the latter case, it is less likely that the efficient level of production (both of the output and pollution) will be achieved. There can also be positive externalities, where one person's actions have an unintended, positive effect on others. Vaccination is an example. People typically get vaccines to protect their own health without taking into consideration that their immunity benefits others.

### *Problems with the Basic Premises*

Satisfying consumer preferences is desirable only if one regards the individual as the fundamental unit of society, as the market does. Those who believe that the common good, however defined, should take precedence over the wants of the individual will not endorse the market system.

The market perception of the individual and the concept of the dignity of the individual are two conflicting views. One would correctly conclude that the market does not respond to or reflect individual human dignity. To do so would require a response to need rather than to want. The market, therefore, cannot *directly* promote a concept of the common good that incorporates notions of human dignity and an option for the poor.

The combination of the sanctity of the individual and the satisfaction of preferences necessarily precludes any judgment concerning the intrinsic merit of the goods that are produced. The market "does not regard any one individual's preferences as less worthy [or less legitimate] than anyone else's, as long as one can pay for one's own satisfactions ... [the market reduces preference] to mere matters of taste, about which it is pointless to dispute" (Anderson, p. 183). The justification "because I want it" is sufficient. The possible result that Worldwide Wrestling is more profitable than opera, because of individual preferences, is of no concern to the market.

The market satisfies consumer wants, not consumer needs. If consumers want filet mignon, ***and can afford it***, then the market will direct resources toward the production of filet mignon even if there are people who are starving. Participants in the market are defined to be those with preferences and income, which excludes a significant portion of the population. This result is consistent with the function of price as creating an incentive. There is a higher reward to resources that satisfy consumer wants, preferences that are backed by income, than consumer needs, which may not be rewarded at all. High-end hotels in Philadelphia that offer room service to guests' dogs provide a dramatic example. "(At the Rittenhouse) Dog owners can choose from five entrees, including beef and bean stew for $18, turkey 'Mutt'loaf' for $16, and 'Mutt'za balls' for $14 that are made with organic chicken and brown rice" (Steele). Across the street, a man sits homeless, begging for something to eat.

This dichotomy between needs and wants is evident as well in the function of price as distributor of income. In a market economy, workers are rewarded according to their contribution to production, which is valued at the market price, independent of any putative intrinsic worth. This is one reason that a home health care worker, who may be perceived as doing something more valuable than a lawyer, earns a considerably lower income.[8]

Distribution of income according to the marginal productivity theory is the antithesis of distribution according to need, so that those who may not need the additional income receive it, while those who may need it do not. Again, we see the role of price as creating incentive. If a worker's income is determined by need, so there is no reward for working harder, taking risks, investing in education and training, there is no incentive to undertake any of these activities. This results in lower output, both quantitatively and qualitatively. "The gap between the rewards to the winners and what is left to the losers must be very large. That is what incentives are all about" (Blinder 1988, p. 27).[9]

### *Justice*

Perhaps the gravest criticism of the market is its inability to do justice. The market results in inequality in the income distribution, with a large disparity between the wealthiest and the poorest. In 2016, the average income of the lowest quintile was about $21, 000. For the highest quintile, it was $291,000, and for the highest 1%, it was $1.8 million.[10] "An unfettered market system shows no mercy" (Blinder 1988, p. 27).

Most economists readily concede this deficiency of the market. In the pursuit of efficiency—producing the most of what consumers want at the least cost—there is a trade-off with equity. It is impossible to reward effort, to create incentive when individuals act in their own self-interest, and at the same time to ensure a minimum standard of living for all in the community within the framework of a free market. For when goods and services are allocated according to need, fewer goods and services are necessarily produced. More equity can be achieved only by sacrificing efficiency.

## Conclusion

When certain conditions are met, the market is efficient; it produces the most goods and services at the lowest cost. It does so because producers and consumers respond to incentives. Firms produce the goods and services consumers want most strongly. "If the fundamental role of an economy is to produce more of the things that people want, anything that conserves on the use of scarce resources is ipso facto desirable" (Blinder 2018, p. 143).

"The market also makes the most of society's limited resources. A free market will assign the highest prices to the scarcest inputs, which will therefore be used sparingly by cost-conscious entrepreneurs. Items in abundant supply will be cheap, and hence use profligately. For the most part, that is how it should be" (Blinder 2018, p. 155).

Price serves multiple functions in a market. When a good or service is not sold to the highest bidder, an alternative way of allocating the product, such as rationing or government mandate, must be used instead.

But there is no question that there are winners and losers in a market economy. That is not only because there are limited resources, but more specifically because self-interested producers have an incentive to produce what consumers want. Only those who are able to participate in the market, which means those who have income to back their preferences, can benefit from it.

The market "will not guarantee distributive justice ... Nothing is wrong with tough competition as long as the weak have some protection from the fallout" (Blinder 2018, p. 159). Economists have long acknowledged that there is a trade-off between equity and efficiency; if a society wants more of one, it will have to give up some of the other.[11] Efficiency is said to measure the size of the economic pie. In that way, there are more goods and services available to be distributed. If society determines that the distribution of goods and services that result from the market is undesirable from a social justice perspective, then it can use other methods (progressive taxes,[12] Pell Grants,[13] or SNAP,[14] for example) to make the income distribution more equitable. If instead of the market, an alternative economic system determines what is produced, there will be fewer goods and services available to redistribute.

## Appendix: Monopoly and Public Goods

Markets achieve efficiency because self-interested individuals provide a constraint on other individuals' self-interest. When there are numerous economic actors in a market, one firm will be unable to raise price above its (efficient) equilibrium level because its rival will offer a lower price to attract consumers. In the case of monopoly, the extreme case of one firm in a market, or oligopoly, the more common instance of just a few firms in the market that can collude to achieve monopoly results, this mechanism breaks down. Such firms are able to raise price without considering a rival's response. The result is price that is higher than and quantity that is lower than the efficient free market levels.

Two policy alternatives address the monopoly problem. The Department of Justice and the Federal Trade Commission enforce the antitrust laws (the Sherman Antitrust Act and Clayton Acts are the major statues[15]). At times, just the threat of such a lawsuit is sufficient to change the firm's anticompetitive behavior. Other times, the penalty in the case results in the necessary changes in structure and/or conduct that restore the workings of the market.[16]

Government regulation replaces the market mechanism when it is impossible to correct the flaws in the particular industry that prevent the efficient market equilibrium from being achieved. These industries are commonly referred to as natural monopolies, characterized by economies of scale. In this case, the efficient price is always less than the average cost, so the firm could not earn a positive profit with a market-determined price. Although the prevalence of price regulation at the national level has decreased significantly since the 1980s, such regulation is more common at the state level for utilities such as electricity, natural gas, and local telephone service, as well as cable television.

A public good is defined to be a good that exhibits the properties of non-rivalrous consumption and non-excludability. Most goods that are exchanged in the market are rivalrous: the more I consume, the less there is for someone else to consume. If I take a piece of pie, there is less pie for anyone else to eat. Watching a movie in a theater is an example of non-rivalrous consumption. I do not use up the movie as I watch it, so there is no additional cost to providing the movie to another viewer (assuming the theater is not full). If anyone who does not pay can be easily excluded from consuming a good, that good is considered to be excludable. A movie is a good example of an excludable good—I can prevent you from entering the theater if you haven't purchased a ticket. Goods that are both non-rivalrous and non-excludable provide benefits to consumers at zero marginal (additional) cost, and no one can be excluded from using them. Consequently, they cannot be produced in a private market, because there is no way to charge a price for them. Such goods are usually provided by the government, and the classic example is national defense.

## Notes

1. In the labor market, the roles are reversed: firms demand the services of labor, and workers supply them.
2. The distinction here between wants and needs is crucial and has implications both for why a market works efficiently and potential objections to the market system. See. Chap. 1 for a discussion.
3. There is considerable discussion of what behavior actually is voluntary. For example, is a woman who becomes a prostitute making a voluntary decision if that is the only way she can earn income? Although selling body organs is illegal in the United States, there is a black market abroad. Are those in extreme poverty making a voluntary decision when they sell one of their kidneys?
4. Sandel describes the market perspective but disagrees that altruism is a scarce commodity. See his discussion in Chapter 4 "How Markets Crowd out Morals" of his book.

5. This example is a different version of one described in Buchholz, p. 22.
6. See Millsap and Boudreaux for a more extensive analysis of the economics of price gouging. Millsap's title, "Price-Gouging Laws—Not Hurricanes—Empty Stores' Shelves" summarizes that perspective.
7. This economic theory is the basis for Chap. 5 on Climate.
8. Marginal productivity is one factor that determines demand for an input. In a competitive input market, the price is determined by demand and supply.
9. See Chapter 18 in Baumol and Blinder for an analysis of the principle of marginal productivity.
10. https://www.cbo.gov/publication/55413.
11. See Okun for a classic analysis of the trade-off.
12. Progressive taxes are defined as taxes that take a higher percentage of income as income increases. Even when taxes are not imposed relative to income, they can be measured in that way. Taxes may also be proportional (the same percent of income regardless of income level) or regressive (a higher percent of income as income increases). For example, a sales tax is a percentage of the price of a good, but because that dollar amount is a higher percentage of a low income, it is a regressive tax.
13. A Pell Grant is federal aid for college that is based on need and awards up to $6000 annually.
14. SNAP is the federal Supplemental Nutrition Assistance Program, more commonly known as food stamps, which provides financial assistance to low-income families to purchase food.
15. https://www.justice.gov/atr/antitrust-laws-and-you.
16. See Irwin M. Stelzer, *Selected Antitrust Cases: Landmark Decisions in Federal Antitrust*, for some of the important antitrust decisions and the remedies imposed.

## Bibliography


Anderson, Elizabeth. "The Ethical Limitations of the Market." *Economics and Philosophy*, 6 (1990), pp. 179–205.

Arrow, Kenneth J. "Gifts and Exchanges." *Philosophy and Public Affairs*, 1, no. 4 (Summer 1972); 343–362.

Barrett, William P. "How to Evaluate a Charity." Forbes, December 12, 2014. https://www.forbes.com/sites/williampbarrett/2016/12/14/how-to-evaluate-a-charity-2/#5845ed213371

Baumol, William J. and Alan S. Blinder. *Microeconomics: Principles and Policy*, Thirteenth Edition. Boston, MA: Cengage Learning, 2016.

Bergdoll, Jonathan; Clark, Chelsea; Xiaonan, Ko; Osili, Una; Coffman, Suzann; Kumar, Supriya; Saronson, Betty; Sato, Grace; Davis-Jones, Melanie; Entcheva, Ruja; Gulliver-Garcia, Tanya; Webster, Regine, "U.S. Household Disaster Giving in 2017 and 2018." IUPUI Scholarly Works. 2019. https://scholarworks.iupui.edu/bitstream/handle/1805/19403/disaster-giving190521.pdf?sequence=1&isAllowed=y

Blinder, Alan. *Hard Heads, Soft Hearts: Tough-minded Economics for a Just Society.* New York, NY: Addison Wesley Publishing Co. Inc., 1988.

Blinder, Alan. *Advice and Dissent: Why America Suffers When Economics and Politics Collide.* New York: Basic Books, 2018.

Boudreaux, Don. "Some Economics of 'Price Gouging'." *Café Hayek* https://cafehayek.com/2015/03/some-economics-of-price-gouging.html

Buchanan, Allen. *Ethics, Efficiency, and the Market.* Totowa, NJ: Rowman and Allanheld, 1985.

Buchholz, Todd G. *New Ideas from Dead Economists: An Introduction to Modern Economic Thought.* London: Plume, 2007.

Friedman, Milton and Rose D. Friedman. *Free to Choose.* New York, NY: Harcourt, Brace, Jovanovic, 1980.

Faculty of the Lilly Family School of Philanthropy. "Eight Myths of US Philanthropy." *Stanford Social Innovation Review,* Fall 2019. https://ssir.org/articles/entry/eight_myths_of_us_philanthropy

Gordon, David and Jeremy Schearmur, editors. *H.B. Acton—The Morals of Markets and Related Essays.* Indianapolis, Indiana: Liberty Fund, 1993

Mankiw, N. Gregory. "I Paid $2,500 for a 'Hamilton' Ticket. I'm Happy About It." *New York Times.* October 21, 2016.

Millsap, Adam. "Price-Gouging Laws—Not Hurricanes—Empty Stores' Shelves." *Forbes*, September 7, 2017. https://www.forbes.com/sites/adammillsap/2017/09/07/price-gouging-laws-not-hurricanes-empty-stores-shelves/#7b2e81c850ce

Okun, Arthur. *Equality and Efficiency: The Big Tradeoff.* Washington, DC: Brookings Institution, 2015.

Schotter, Andrew. *Free Market Economics, A Critical Appraisal.* B. Blackwell, 1990.

Steele, Allison. "Going to the dogs: At some Philadelphia hotels, you can order fancy room service for your pooch." *Philadelphia Inquirer*, May 13, 2019. https://www.inquirer.com/food/restaurants/dog-room-service-rittenhouse-hotel-ritz-carlton-four-seasons-luxury-20190513.html

Walt, Vivienne, "Rising from the Ashes: Inside the fight over rebuilding Notre Dame." *Time*, August 5, 2019, pp. 31–40. https://time.com/5634240/notre-dame-fire-france-battle/

CHAPTER 3

# Minimum Wage/Living Wage

**Abstract** This chapter begins with a historical review of the federal minimum wage and data about minimum wage. The current federal minimum wage is $7.25 an hour and hasn't been increased in 10 years. Twenty-nine states have a minimum wage higher than the federal one. An economic analysis of the minimum wage follows with a review of the empirical research.

The next section is a discussion of the Jewish social justice perspective. The Jewish tradition views the worker as a human person, who should be paid sufficiently to support a family. In fact, an employer is considered to be responsible for the welfare of workers, a direct contradiction of standard economic analysis. I conclude with a discussion of the $15 minimum wage movement.

**Keywords** Minimum wage • Economic analysis • Human person

## Introduction

Generally, economists oppose government interference with the market because it leads to inefficiencies. It is particularly significant that for decades, one of the few things that economists agreed about was that the minimum wage is an ill-advised policy. In a 2007 survey, a majority of labor economists agreed that "minimum wage hikes are an inefficient way to address the needs of poor families."[1] In another survey, almost 80% of economists replied that increasing the minimum wage would increase



N. R. Fox, *Profits and Prophets*,
https://doi.org/10.1007/978-3-030-40556-4_3

unemployment among unskilled and young workers (Mankiw).[2] Path-breaking research in the 1990s, though, changed that view.

Discussion of minimum wage informs important concepts of social justice, people as workers and how economists view them, and what should determine a person's wage. Views on poverty, charity, human dignity, and the value of work all inform the Jewish ethical perspective.

In this chapter, I will discuss the theory of wage determination in general and minimum wage in particular, the long-standing empirical work, and the most recent empirical work, which has changed economic thinking. Then I will discuss Jewish teaching on wages and how to treat the worker, which connects to the $15 wage movement.

## Economic Analysis

As with most regulations that interfere with the market mechanism, imposition of a minimum wage is usually well-intended. And like most such regulations, it may in fact harm the very group it is intended to help. The theory of wage determination predicts that the number of workers hired will decrease as the minimum wage is increased. But that conclusion is very general and is based on assumptions that have come into question.

Economists view workers as just one part of the production process, who should be paid according to their productivity.[3] Firms will pay the lowest wage possible as long as they can get the quantity and quality of workers they want in order to keep their costs as low as possible. In this economic view, workers are no different from any other input—lumber, electricity, flour—so an increase in the minimum wage with no corresponding increase in productivity makes no sense. More significantly, and in direct contrast with Jewish social teaching, there is no regard for how the wage level affects the worker as a human person or whether it is sufficient to his/her need.

The economic theory of the minimum wage is straightforward. Wage is the price of labor. Minimum wage, by construction, is higher than the equilibrium wage.[4] The result is an excess supply of labor—more workers are willing to work at that higher than equilibrium wage than firms are willing to hire. The Law of Demand[5] states that if the price of something increases, people demand less of it. If wage increases, then firms will demand fewer workers. Of course, those who are employed at the higher wage are better off, but the same cannot be true of people who are willing to work at the higher wage but are not hired. Even if the firm would continue to hire the same number of workers, that would mean their costs increase. Either their profits fall, or they raise their prices. Economic theory predicts that there would be some adverse effect—fewer workers hired, higher prices and/or lower profits. Economic studies confirmed this theory for many years.[6] They found that as minimum wage was increased, employment fell. And for decades, this was the accepted, prevailing wisdom in the profession—until about 25 years ago.

In the mid-1990s, Card and Krueger conducted a study comparing employment in fast-food restaurants in Pennsylvania and New Jersey. They were fortunate to have found what economists call a "natural" experiment—two contiguous states with different levels of the minimum wage. They found that employment grew faster in New Jersey, which had increased its minimum wage, than it had in Pennsylvania, whose state minimum wage remained unchanged. These results contradicted decades of research (Card and Krueger 1994).

Why the change from earlier research? In part, because at that time, the minimum wage was so low, relative to the average wage, the increase affected many fewer workers. The percentage of workers earning at or below the minimum wage had fallen dramatically; it was 15% in 1980; it fell to 7.7% in 1992 (BLS 2015). That number has fallen to 2.1% in 2018 (BLS 2018). Another difference is that now minimum wage workers are concentrated in the service industries, especially food, hospitality, and health care (Pew). It is very difficult to find a substitute for a hotel housekeeper. Subsequent studies also found that increases in minimum wage have a net positive effect (Tedeschi).[7]

## History of the Minimum Wage in the United States

The 1938 Fair Labor Standards Act established a federal minimum wage as well as laws governing hours worked (maximum of 44 per week) and child labor (Grossman).[8] The 25 cent per hour minimum covered only 11 million workers (Elder and Miller, p. 10). Sec. 202(a) of the Act states that "labor conditions detrimental to the maintenance of the minimum standard of living necessary for health, efficiency, and general well-being of workers" had negative effects on the economy, including unfair competition and interference with the free flow of goods and services (Fair Labor Standards Act).

Even at that time, there were concerns about the effect of a minimum wage on the economy. In a fireside chat, President Roosevelt said "do not let any calamity-howling executive with an income of $1000 a day, ... tell you ... that a wage of $11 a week is going to have a disastrous effect on all American industry" (Roosevelt, p. 392).

The federal minimum wage has been increased over 20 times since 1938. The most recent increase was in 2009. In 2007, the federal minimum wage was increased for the first time in 10 years.[9] It increased from $5.15 an hour to $5.85. It went up each year until it reached $7.25 in July 2009, its current level.

Although the federal minimum wage is the highest it has ever been in nominal terms, in terms of buying power, it is lower than it has been since the mid-1960s.[10] Even though today's federal minimum wage workers earn more dollars than their counterparts in 1968, today's workers are actually worse off. In 1968, the federal minimum wage was $1.60, the equivalent of $11.55 in 2018.[11]

Who earns the minimum wage in 2018? About 75% are white, 21% are aged 16–19, about 50% are female, and 75% work full-time. Seen from a different perspective, of all teenagers (ages 16–19) earning an hourly wage, 7.6% earn at or below the federal minimum wage. That figure is 2.6% for women and 2.6% for African Americans. About 1.7 million workers total earn at or below the (federal) minimum wage.[12] The percentage of hourly paid workers earning the prevailing federal minimum wage or less declined from 2.3% in 2017 to 2.1% in 2018. This remains well below the percentage of 13.4 recorded in 1979, when data for hourly paid were first collected on a regular basis.[13]

There is another way to put the minimum wage in perspective. Someone working full-time at the current federal minimum wage of $7.25 earns not quite $15,080 annually, which is below the poverty threshold of about $25,000 for a family of four per the revised guidelines of 2019.[14] Nowhere in the United States does a minimum wage worker earn enough in a 40-hour work week to rent a modest, affordable,[15] two-bedroom apartment (Cooper). In over 15 states, workers would need to earn over $20 an hour, almost three times the current federal minimum wage, for that apartment.[16]

Congress considered several proposals to increase the federal minimum wage in 2010 (CBO 2014, p. 6). These included a three-step increase from the (then) current level of $7.25 to $10.10, with the wage indexed to inflation and $9.00, and a two-step increase from $7.25 to $9.00, with no index. No legislation was passed. In 2014, the Congressional Budget Office (CBO) published an analysis of the effects of both of these scenarios on the economy. They concluded that total employment would fall by about 500,000 workers, but more than 16.5 million workers would have a higher salary. About 19% of the $31 billion pay increase would go to families below the poverty line, and 29% to families at or above three times the poverty line (CBO, 2014, pp. 2–3).

## Fight for $15 Movement

In 2012, out of frustration with the lack of progress in increasing the federal minimum wage, fast-food workers held a one-day strike in support of a $15 minimum wage (Greenhouse). There was widespread skepticism that a more than 100% increase in the minimum wage would be realized. Yet less than four years later, both California and New York had enacted legislation that would increase their respective minimum wages to $15 by 2022 (California) and $15 by 2018 (New York City), 2021 (New York City suburbs), and $12.50 in upstate New York (Greenhouse). Twenty-nine states plus the District of Columbia have higher minimum wages than the federal $7.25.[17] Washington, D.C., is the highest at $13.25. The highest state minimum wages of $13.25 are in Massachusetts and Washington.[18] Workers are entitled to the higher of the two when the state minimum wage is higher than the federal rate.[19] In February 2017, Governor Tom Wolf of Pennsylvania proposed raising the state minimum wage from the current (federal level) of $7.25 to $12.00 (Thompson). A recent survey reported that about 60% of Americans polled support the increase to $15 (Greenhouse).

In the past few years, several major firms announced that they would increase hourly pay to workers to a level significantly higher than the federal minimum wage. In 2016, JPMorgan Chase announced its minimum wage would be $10.15, increasing to $16.50 by 2020. CEO Jamie Dimon described the decision as "the right thing to do" and good for the company (Dimon). Other firms soon followed, including major retailers Amazon ($15), Costco ($14), Target ($13), Walmart ($11), and CVS ($11). Some plan to raise that minimum even higher by 2020 (Sciproni). As the recovery from the 2008 recession continues and the unemployment rate falls, firms need to increase wages to attract workers. At the same time, they have found that turnover, a significant labor cost, falls as wages increase (Pinsker).[20]

Economists at the University of Washington found Seattle's recent minimum wage increases brought benefits to many workers employed at the time, while leaving few employed workers worse off.[21] In a revision of that study, they found that average pay fell by about $125 a month (Scheiber). They concluded that an increase in minimum wage has different effects on different groups of workers, helping those already in low-paying jobs but hurting those not yet employed (Ekaterina et. al.). In a simulation of the effect of a $15 minimum wage in Washington, D.C., researchers predict that the lowest wage earners will see a significant increase in income with relatively small job losses (Muhammad 2018).

## Jewish Social Justice

The Jewish texts teach about God's view of both those in need and those who do not treat them in a fair and just manner, about the employer/employee relationship, and the importance of preventing poverty in the first place by providing for a worker's needs. The worker is a person, a creation of God, entitled to human dignity and respect. People need to work in order to acquire goods and services—"By the sweat of your brow shall you get bread to eat …" (Genesis 3:19). The purpose of work is to earn a living, so the purpose of a wage is to provide a living. Workers should be paid according to their needs. This perspective is in direct contrast with the market view of workers.

Workers are not just another input; they are human beings, and employers have some responsibility for their employees' well-being. Work is holy because it is a way to partner with God in the act of creation. Poverty is something to be avoided, and although we are commanded to help those in need, the preferred way is to prevent poverty in the first place.[22] "Do not let him slip down until he falls completely, for then it will be difficult to raise him; rather strengthen him as he begins to fall" (Dorff, p. 34). It is an affront to human dignity to work full-time and still be poor. The purpose of work is to earn a living, so it follows logically that the purpose of a wage is to provide a living (Jacobs 2008, p. 23).

What does God think of those who do not treat their workers in a just way? "[A]nd I will act as a relentless accuser against those who have no fear of Me: Who practice sorcery, who commit adultery, who swear falsely, **who cheat laborers of their hire**, … said the Lord of Hosts" (Malachi 3:5, emphasis mine). "He who withholds what is due the poor affronts his Maker; He who shows pity for the needy honors Him" (Proverbs 14:31).

What do we learn from these verses? First, a worker is someone who is vulnerable and needs protection. "The principle 'you should keep the ways of the righteous' compels employers to recognize their privileged and powerful position vis-à-vis their workers, and to act in such a way as to protect the interests of the workers" (Jacobs 2008, p. 13). As we see from the prophet Malachi, a worker is in the same category as the widow, the orphan, and the stranger.[23] He is at the mercy of his employer; when we consider a minimum wage worker, it is easy to see the imbalance of power between him and his employer. God considers anyone who mistreats the stranger and the immigrant in the same category as adulterers and blasphemers. Whoever does not look out for the welfare of the worker, and the employer who pays the worker a sub-standard wage, is mistreating the worker, and thus is included in the same category as adulterers and blasphemers. Similarly, as Proverbs 14:31 teaches, that same person is dishonoring God.

Citing "those who cheat labors of their hire," perhaps the prophet Malachi had in mind the biblical verse that commands an employer to pay his workers on time. "You must pay his wages on the same day, before the sun sets, for he is needy and urgently depends on it; else he will cry to the Lord against you and you will incur guilt" (Deuteronomy 24:15).

No ATMs, smart phones, microwaves back then. The pressing labor issue of that time was prompt payment of wages (Jacobs, p. 44). Workers needed their wages daily in order to buy food and other necessities of life. In this view, the employer has a *moral* responsibility for the well-being of the worker (Jacobs 2003, p. 44). If tardy payment can produce such dire consequences, it must also be the case the insufficient wages would have the same result.

In his commentary on this verse, Nahmanides writes, "For he is poor—like the majority of hired laborers, and he depends on the wages to buy food by which to live ... if he does not collect the wages right away as he is leaving work, he will go home, and his wages will remain with you until the morning, and he will die of hunger that night" (Jacobs 2003, p. 45). The employer is responsible for the employee's well-being. If the worker and/or his family die of hunger as a result of non-payment of wages, Nahmanides implies, fault for the death lies with the employer (Jacobs 2003, p. 45).

If the employer is bound to pay on time for the sake of the well-being of the worker, he must be obligated to pay a living wage for the same reason. To revise this biblical verse to make it contemporary, "You must *pay* him a wage sufficient for his needs ... For he is needy and depends upon it." In addressing the issue most relevant to workers of its own time (paying on time), the Bible invites us to consider ways to ameliorate the situation of workers in our own time. Paying workers promptly constitutes only one means of fulfilling the more general commandment, “do not oppress the hired laborer” (Jacobs 2008, pp. 21–22). This perspective is entirely absent from the economic model of wage determination, where the employer bears no personal responsibility for the worker at all.

Rules for charity can also guide us on the Jewish social ethics perspective on the minimum wage. “You shall open your hand [to the poor person] and provide him *sufficient for his need, whatever it might be*” (Deuteronomy 15:8). Even though this is a reference to how much charity you should give, it clearly has application to the minimum/living wage issue. For if you are to *give* a poor person enough charity for his needs, does it not follow that you ought to *pay* him enough for his needs if he is working? (Jacobs 2008, p. 23).

In Maimonides’ rules for charity, the highest form of charity is to enable someone to be self-sufficient, so he no longer needs to depend on the generosity of others.[24] Surely the best way to ensure that someone is self-sufficient is to pay a living wage.

We can infer rabbinic thinking on a living wage from their discussion of business profits.[25] They recognize that people respond to incentives, and the Talmud has much to say about the market and business practices. Rabbis set a maximum rate on profits, so that essential goods remained affordable. This profit ceiling is, essentially, a limited form of price control grounded in economic justice and a dose of market reality. Wage is the price of labor, so we can extend that Talmudic reasoning as support for a living wage sufficient to support a worker’s needs.

Maimonides allows us to make a connection between wage and worker productivity. Workers have an obligation to their employers in the sense of a day’s work. “Just as the employer must be careful not to steal the salary of the poor [worker], so too must the poor person be careful not to steal the work of the owner by wasting a little time here and there until the entire day is filled with trickery” (*Mishne Torah, Hilkhot Skhirut 13:7, cf. Shulhan Arukh, Hoshen Mishpat* 337:20 quoted in Jacobs 2003, p. 46). Workers are also prohibited from working both a day and a night job, as working double shifts interferes with one’s ability to perform either job well (Jacobs, p. 46).

Could we interpret this teaching to conclude that a worker who “fills his days with trickery” or who holds two jobs and so is too tired to be as productive as if he would otherwise be, should be paid less? And if that seems logical, that the wage should be tied to productivity, perhaps that implies that there should be no increase in minimum wage if there is no increase in productivity?

Paying a just wage also contributes to the dignity of the worker. For just as the community has obligations to the poor, the poor have obligations to the community. Even those who live entirely on charity are required to donate to another poor person (Dorff, p. 28). They are expected to contribute to the community—how better to accomplish that than by providing a just wage to those who are working?[26]

## Conclusion

For decades, most economists made the case against the minimum wage, and the data supported the theory that increasing the minimum wage would decrease employment among low-paid workers. At the same time, those concerned with Jewish social justice argued in favor of a higher minimum wage, relying on biblical and rabbinic teachings. Changes in the economy and changes in the labor market have resulted in a prevailing market wage in many sectors that is above the current federal minimum wage. Almost 60% of states have a minimum wage higher than the federal, and several major companies have voluntarily increased the wage they pay their lowest paid workers to a level above the federal minimum wage. Jewish social ethics has consistently called for a living wage. Achieving a living wage as the law of the land will require "reconstructing modern values so that human beings are no longer viewed as economic or political instruments to be used or discarded at will. Employment (at a living wage) brings with it not only self-esteem but the esteem of others ..." (Dorff, p. 36).

## Notes

1. https://www.epionline.org/release/majority-of-labor-economists-believe-minimum-wage-hikes-cause-unemployment/.
2. Significantly, both of these surveys were in the 2000s, when most increases in the minimum wage would have been incremental, unlike the increase to $15 that is being considered in 2019.
3. Productivity affects the demand for workers. In the market, equilibrium wage is determined by both supply and demand.

4. There is no purpose to having a minimum wage higher than the market wage. When the price floor is below the equilibrium, Mankiw calls it "non-binding."
5. See Chap. 2 for a fuller discussion of the Law of Demand and the effect of price ceilings.
6. See Brown and Brown et al. for a review of earlier studies. A comprehensive list of research on the minimum wage can be found in Appendix B in CBO (2019).
7. Other studies find no significant negative employment effect when states raised minimum wages (Tedeschi). He also reports that teenage employment rose as much in states that increased their minimum wage as in states that did not.
8. See https://www.dol.gov/whd/regs/compliance/hrg.htm#1 for details about current implementation and rules.
9. http://www.minimum-wage.org/minimum-wage-raise.
10. https://www.cnbc.com/2016/07/21/adjusted-for-inflation-the-federal-minimum-wage-is-worth-less-than-50-years-ago.html.
11. https://www.cnn.com/interactive/2019/business/us-minimum-wage-by-year/index.html.
12. https://www.bls.gov/opub/reports/minimum-wage/2018/pdf/home.pdf.
13. https://www.bls.gov/opub/reports/minimum-wage/2018/pdf/home.pdf.
14. https://www.healthcare.gov/glossary/federal-poverty-level-FPL/.
15. The U.S. Department of Housing and Urban Development defines "affordable" as 30% or less of monthly income (Cooper).
16. https://reports.nlihc.org/oor.
17. https://www.dol.gov/whd/minwage/america.htm.
18. In New York, the minimum wage will be $15 in New York City, Long Island, and West Chester County by 2021 and $12.50 in other parts of the state(https://www.ny.gov/new-york-states-minimum-wage/new-york-states-minimum-wage).
19. https://www.dol.gov/general/topic/wages/minimumwage.
20. Some studies find that it can cost a company about 20% of annual salary to replace a worker (Boushey and Glynn), though the number is likely significantly lower for the lowest paid employees.
21. Seattle increased its minimum wage for large employers to $11 an hour, from $9.47, in April 2015, then to $13 for many of those same employers in January 2016 (Scheiber).
22. Based on Leviticus 25:35, "if your kinsman stumbles." Commentary Rabbinical Assembly, *Etz Hayim*, p. 743.
23. See also Jacobs ( 2008, p. 20).

24. See Salamon for a very accessible discussion of Rambam's Ladder.
25. See Chap. 2 for a discussion of profit ceilings.
26. See Dorff (p. 44) for a discussion of the mutual obligations of the community and the poor.

## Bibliography


Boushey, Heather and Sarah Jane Glynn. "There Are Significant Business Costs to Replacing Employees." Center for American Progress. November 16, 2012. https://www.americanprogress.org/wp-content/uploads/2012/11/CostofTurnover.pdf

Brown, Charles. "Minimum Wages, Employment, and the Distribution of Income," in Orley C. Ashenfelter and David Card, eds., *Handbook of Labor Economics,* vol. 3, part B (Elsevier, 1999), pp. 2101–2163. https://econpapers.repec.org/bookchap/eeelabchp/3-32.htm

Brown, Charles, Curtis Gilroy, and Andrew Kohen. "The Effect of the Minimum Wage on Employment and Unemployment," *Journal of Economic Literature,* vol. 20, no. 2 (June 1982), pp. 487–528. www.jstor.org/stable/2724487

BLS. https://www.bls.gov/opub/reports/minimum-wage/2015/home.htm

BLS. https://www.bls.gov/opub/reports/minimum-wage/2018/home.htm

BLS Wage and Hour Division. https://www.dol.gov/whd/minwage/america.htm

Card, David and Alan Krueger. "Minimum Wages and Employment: A Case Study of the Fast-Food Industry in New Jersey and Pennsylvania." *American Economic Review.* ER Vol. 84, No. 4 9/94, pp. 772–793, 1994.

CBO. *The Effects of a Minimum-Wage Increase on Employment and Family Income.* February 2014. https://www.cbo.gov/sites/default/files/113th-congress-2013-2014/reports/44995-MinimumWage_OneColumn.pdf

CBO. *The Effects on Employment and Family Income of Increasing the Federal Minimum Wage.* July 2019. https://www.cbo.gov/system/files/2019-07/CBO-55410-MinimumWage2019.pdf

CNBC.com. http://www.cnbc.com/2016/07/12/jamie-dimon-on-why-hes-giving-jpmorgan-employees-a-raise.html

Cooper, Gael F. "How much do you need to earn to afford an apartment in each state?" Gael F. Cooper MSN Money Talks News, September 28, 2018. https://www.msn.com/en-us/money/realestate/how-much-do-you-need-to-earn-to-afford-an-apartment-in-each-state/ss-BBNFa6d

Department of Labor, Wage and Hour Division. https://www.dol.gov/whd/state/stateMinWageHis.htm

Department of Labor General Topics. https://www.dol.gov/general/topic/wages/minimumwage

Department of Labor Minimum Wage Chart. https://www.dol.gov/whd/state/stateMinWageHis.htm

DePillis, Lydia. "The Profit Motive behind Wal-Mart's minimum wage hike." *The Washington Post*, February 19, 2015. https://www.washingtonpost.com/news/wonk/wp/2015/02/19/the-profit-motive-behind-walmarts-minimum-wage-hike/?utm_term=.b9601e8e4bbb

Dimon, Jamie. "Why We're Giving our Employees a Raise." *New York Times*. July 12, 2016. https://www.nytimes.com/2016/07/12/opinion/jamie-dimon-why-were-giving-our-employees-a-raise.html

Dorff, Elliot N. "Jewish Perspectives on the Poor." *The Poor Among Us. Jewish Tradition and Social Policy*. The American Jewish Committee, 1986.

Elder, Peyton K. and Heidi D. Miller. "The Fair Labor Standards Act: Changes of four decades." *Monthly Labor Review*, July 1, 1979, pp. 10–16.

Fair Labor Standards Act of 1938. https://www.dol.gov/sites/dolgov/files/WHD/legacy/files/FairLaborStandAct.pdf

Favre, Lauren. "Minimum Wage Workers Cannot Afford Housing." *U.S. News and World Report*, June 20, 2019. https://www.usnews.com/news/best-states/articles/2019-06-20/minimum-wage-workers-still-cant-afford-housing-report-shows

Greenhouse, Steven. "How the $15 Minimum Wage Went from Laughable to Viable." *New York Times*, April 1, 2016. https://www.nytimes.com/2016/04/03/sunday-review/how-the-15-minimum-wage-went-from-laughable-to-viable.html?_r=0

Grossman, Jonathan. "Fair Labor Standards Act of 1938: Maximum Struggle for a Minimum Wage." *Monthly Labor Review*, June 1978. https://www.dol.gov/general/aboutdol/history/flsa1938

Healthcare.gov. https://www.healthcare.gov/glossary/federal-poverty-level-FPL/

Jacobs, Rabbi Jill. "The Living Wage: A Jewish Approach." *Conservative Judaism*. Spring 2003, pp. 38–51.

Jacobs, Rabbi Jill. "Work, workers, and the Jewish owner." The Rabbinical Assembly, May 28, 2008. http://www.rabbinicalassembly.org/sites/default/files/public/halakhah/teshuvot/20052010/jacobs-living-wage.pdf?phpMyAdmin=G0Is7ZE%2CH7O%2Ct%2CZ1sDHpI8UAVD6

Jardim, Ekaterina, Mark C. Long, Robert Plotnick, Emma van Inwegen, Jacob Vigdor, Hilary Wething. "Minimum Wage Increases and Individual Employment Trajectories." NBER Program(s): Labor Studies. NBER Working Paper No. 25182, October 2018. https://www.nber.org/papers/w25182?utm_campaign=ntw&utm_medium=email&utm_source=ntwg20

Kurtz, Annalyn, Tal Yellin and Will Houp. "The US minimum wage through the years." CNN Business. April 9, 2019. https://www.cnn.com/interactive/2019/business/us-minimum-wage-by-year/index.html

Labor Center Berkeley. http://laborcenter.berkeley.edu/minimum-wage-living-wage-resources/inventory-of-us-city-and-county-minimum-wage-ordinances/

Mankiw, N. Gregory *Principles of Microeconomics*, 8th Edition. Boston: Cengage, 2017.

Minimum-Wage.org. http://www.minimum-wage.org/minimum-wage-raise

Muhammad, Daniel "Earnings, EITC, and Employment Responses to a $15 Minimum Wage: Will Low-Income Workers Be Better Off?" Under review *Economic Development Quarterly*, 2018.

Owens, Christie. "Wal-Mart CAN afford a $15 Wage." CNBC June 3, 2016. http://www.cnbc.com/2016/06/03/walmart-can-afford-15-minimum-wage-commentary.html

National Low Income Housing Coalition. *Out of Reach: The High Cost of Housing 2018*. https://reports.nlihc.org/sites/default/files/oor/OOR_2018.pdf

Pew. http://www.pewresearch.org/fact-tank/2014/09/08/who-makes-minimum-wage/

Pinsker, Joe. "Why Walmart Raised its Wage." *The Atlantic*. February 19, 2015. https://www.theatlantic.com/business/archive/2015/02/why-walmart-raised-its-wages/385670/

Ritholtz, Barry. "Wal-Mart's Minimum Wage Breakdown." *Bloomberg View*. February 23, 2015. https://www.bloomberg.com/view/articles/2015-02-23/wal-mart-raises-minimum-wage-as-laws-change-labor-gets-scarce

Roosevelt, Franklin. *Public Papers and Address*, Vol. VII New York: Random House, 1937.

Salamon, Julie. *Rambam's Ladder: A Meditation on Generosity and Why It Is Necessary to Give*. Workman Publishing Company, 2003.

Scheiber, Noam. "They Said Seattle's Higher Base Pay Would Hurt Workers. Why Did They Flip?" *New York Times*, October 22, 2018. https://www.nytimes.com/2018/10/22/business/economy/seattle-minimum-wage-study.html

Scipioni, Jade. "Minimum wage on the rise, these companies are in the lead." Fox Business, April 4, 2019. https://www.foxbusiness.com/retail/amazon-walmart-costco-target-highest-minimum-wage

Selyukh, Alina. "$15 Minimum Wage Would Boost 17 Million Workers, Cut 1.3 Million Jobs, CBO Says." NPR, July 8, 2019. https://www.npr.org/2019/07/08/739607964/-15-minimum-wage-would-boost-17-million-workers-cut-1-3-million-jobs-cbo-says

Stolberg, Sheryl Gay and Jeanna Smialek. "House Passes Bill to Raise Minimum Wage to $15, a Victory for Liberals." *New York Times*, July 18, 2019. https://www.nytimes.com/2019/07/18/us/politics/minimum-wage.html

Swanson, Ana. "What you'd need to earn in every state to rent a decent apartment." *The Washington Post*, June 8, 2015. https://www.washingtonpost.com/news/wonk/wp/2015/06/09/what-youd-need-to-earn-in-every-state-to-afford-a-decent-apartment/?utm_term=.5f0f1b5623bf

*Tanakh: A New Translation of the Holy Scriptures According to Traditional Hebrew Text*. Philadelphia, Jewish Publication Society, 1985.

Tankersley, Jim and Emily Cochrane. "$15 Minimum Wage Would Reduce Poverty but Cost Jobs, Congress Told in Report." *New York Times*, July 8, 2019. https://www.nytimes.com/2019/07/08/us/politics/federal-minimum-wage.html?auth=login-email&login=email

Tedeschi, Ernie. "Americans Are Seeing Highest Minimum Wage in History (Without Federal Help)." *New York Times*, April 29, 2019. https://www.nytimes.com/2019/04/24/upshot/why-america-may-already-have-its-highest-minimum-wage.html

Thompson, Charles. "Gov. Tom Wolf kick-starts Pennsylvania minimum wage debate with bold budget." *PA Penn Live*. February 7, 2017. http://www.pennlive.com/politics/index.ssf/2017/02/gov_tom_wolf_kick-starts_minim.html

U.S. Department of Labor, Wage and Hours Division. "History of Federal Minimum Wage Rates Under the Fair Labor Standards Act, 1938–2009." https://www.dol.gov/whd/minwage/chart.htm

Weise, Karen. "Amazon to Raise Minimum Wage to $15 for All U.S. Workers. *New York Times*. October 2, 2018. https://www.nytimes.com/2018/10/02/business/amazon-minimum-wage.html

CHAPTER 4

# Immigration

**Abstract** This chapter begins with a historical overview and continues with the effects of immigration on the economy in general and on native wages. Standard economic theory predicts that as immigrants increase the supply of labor, equilibrium wage will decrease. Most studies conclude that there is minimal effect on native wages, mostly on workers in low-skilled jobs without a high school education.

Economic research also shows that the impact of immigration changes over time. Immigrants add to federal revenues but are generally a cost at the state and local level. The last section examines Jewish teaching. Loving the stranger is a basic Jewish value; the *ger* (stranger) should be protected. The market and Jewish social justice perspectives both support a generous, pro-immigrant public policy.

**Keywords** Immigration • Native wages • *Ger*-Stranger

> *You shall love the stranger, for you were strangers in the land of Egypt.* (Deuteronomy 10:19)



N. R. Fox, *Profits and Prophets*,
https://doi.org/10.1007/978-3-030-40556-4_4

## Introduction

How should we determine immigration policy? Should the economic impact be the primary factor or are the ethical factors—"give me your tired, your poor"—more important? Immigration was a crucial election-year issue in the 2016 presidential election. With the end of DACA[1] and President Trump's recent proposal to change immigration policy from family based to merit based,[2] it remains a critical political and economic issue. The effect of immigration is an important topic in economics, especially as it relates to the supply of labor and its effect on wages. And certainly, concern for those at the margin, for the *ger*, the stranger, is a critical topic in Jewish social justice.

This chapter begins with results from public opinion surveys about immigration and its effect in the United States, in general and on the economy in particular. Historical data about immigration follows, including a brief summary of U.S. policy. I then present economic analysis of the effect of immigration. "Economists generally agree that the effects of immigration on the U.S. economy are broadly positive."[3] The Jewish social justice perspective concludes the chapter.

## Public Opinion

Public opinion about immigration provides a context for economic and social justice analysis. In a 2019 poll, a majority (62%) replied that "immigrants strengthen the country because of their hard work and talents." Just 28% said that "immigrants are a burden on the country because they take jobs, housing and health care." The results were almost exactly the opposite about 25 years earlier (Jones).

Gallop reports more specific results. A June 2018 poll showed that 75% of those surveyed believe that immigration is a good thing for the country; 19% think it is bad. A June 2017 poll showed that 45% think immigration has made the economy better; 30% believe it has made it worse; and 22% see little significant effect. That same poll found that 18% believe immigrants take low-paying jobs that native workers want, while 72% believe they take low-paying jobs that native workers do not want. A 2019 poll found that 23% would like immigration to decrease; 15% would like to see an increase.[4]

Two results stand out from these surveys. Even though almost three-quarters of those polled believe that immigration is good for the United

States, only about one-sixth favor an increase in immigration. About one-fifth of those polled believe that immigrants "steal" jobs from Americans, but those voices seem to be the loudest in the debate.

## Immigration by the Numbers

Immigration has fluctuated significantly over the past 150 years. In 1850, there were about 2 million immigrants,[5] accounting for about 10% of the population. Those numbers increased through 1930 (14 million, 11.6%), then fell through 1970 (9 million, 4.7%). They have been increasing steadily since to 44 million immigrants, 13.5% of the population in 2017 (Migration Policy Institute [MPI], U.S. Immigrant Population and Share over Time, 1850–present).

Immigration (new immigrants arriving each year) was below one million throughout the 1800s. It fell in the first half of the twentieth century (to a low of 20,000–30,000 before the end of World War II). Since then, the number has steadily increased. So far in the last decade, the average was just over one million a year.[6] As a percent of the population, immigrants are at about the same level as they were in the late nineteenth and early twentieth centuries.[7]

The geographic origin of immigrants has changed as well. In 1960, over 70% were from Europe and 20% from the Americas. After "Other," most immigrants came from Italy, 12.9%, and 5.9% came from Mexico. In 2017, about half were from the Americas, 30% from Asia, and 10% from Europe (MPI). After "Other," most immigrants came from Mexico (25.3%); Italy did not even appear as a separate country of origin (MPI, "Regions of Birth for Immigrants in the United States, 1960–Present").

Educational achievement of immigrants has also changed. In 1960, 75% of immigrants had not graduated from high school, 14% had only a high school diploma, and just over 10% had any higher education. In 2016, 29% had not graduated from high school, 22% had a high school diploma, and over half had some higher education.[8] In 2016, almost 50% of immigrants had a high school diploma or less, while that number was just under a third for native-born Americans. At the other extreme of the education spectrum, college degree and beyond, the numbers are comparable, at about a third.[9]

## Timeline of Immigration Laws

Immigration laws were first enacted in the United States soon after independence. The 1790 Naturalization Act limited citizenship to "free white" immigrants of good moral character. The Chinese Exclusion Act (1882) was the first of several laws that severely limited Chinese immigration. The National Origins Quota Act (1924, known as the Johnson-Reed Act) established quotas based on country of national origin. A maximum of 2% of each nationality, based on the 1890 Census, were permitted to enter the United States. This law significantly affected immigration from southern and eastern Europe. The Immigration Nationality Act (1952, known as the McCarran-Walter Act) preserved the quota system but modified the rules.

It was not until 1965, with the passage of the 1965 Immigration and Nationality Act (known as the Hart-Celler Act) that the quota system was abolished and replaced with a system based on family unification.[10] In 2019, President Trump proposed a new immigration policy that would severely cut back the importance of family unification (though he does prioritize immediate family members, spouses, and children [Trump]). He would replace those criteria with skills, education, and human capital (Trump, Shear). Though he has not yet presented details, his proposal is similar to RAISE (Reforming American Immigration for Stronger Employment) that three Republican senators introduced in the Senate in April 2019 (Bolton). One of the provisions of an earlier version of that proposed legislation would establish immigration based on a score on a test that includes questions about education, English proficiency, age, and whether you had won a Nobel Prize or Olympic medal.[11]

## Immigrants as Part of the U.S. Labor Force

Foreign-born workers accounted for nearly 17% (28.0 million) of the 162.1 million workers in the civilian labor force in 2018 (United States Department of Labor, BLS Table 1). The median usual weekly earnings of foreign-born full-time wage and salary workers were $758 in 2018, compared with $910 for their native-born counterparts (United States Department of Labor, BLS Table 5). Differences in earnings reflect a variety of factors, including differences in educational achievement, occupation, and geographic region. Hispanics accounted for about half of the foreign-born labor force in 2016, and Asians accounted for about a quarter (United States Department of Labor, BLS, Table 5).

Foreign-born workers were more likely than native-born workers to be employed in service occupations; natural resources, construction, and maintenance occupations; and production, transportation, and material moving occupations. Native-born workers were more likely than foreign-born workers to be employed in management, professional, and related occupations and sales and office occupations (BLS Table 4). The difference can be attributed primarily to training and education and most significantly to language skills.

## Economic Effects of Immigration

Economists who embrace a free market (efficiency as a goal, producing as much as possible with scarce resources) would argue for as few restrictions on the flow of labor as possible, in much the same way they argue for minimal trade restrictions, such as tariffs and quotas, on imported goods. The effect of immigration on various sectors of the economy and on native wages and employment should both be considered when evaluating immigration policy. This includes effects on native wages, prices of goods and services, and government revenue.

## Effect on Native Wages and Jobs

There is a consensus over years of research that the effect of immigration on native wages and jobs is minimal and primarily on low-skilled jobs (Wharton, Orrenius). The studies' results of the effect of immigration on native wages range from –1.7% to +1.7% for workers with no high school diploma, with larger effects on immigrants who are already working (Wharton). For all workers, regardless of educational attainment, these numbers are 0.6% change in wages for native workers and an average –5% for immigrants who are already working (Wharton). Overall, the evidence that immigrants have harmed the opportunities of less-educated natives is scant (Card).

## Skilled Workers

There is evidence that skilled workers benefit directly from immigrant labor in the form of more jobs, and skilled workers are disproportionately natives (Orrenius). This is because in many instances, unskilled immigrant labor is a complement for skilled labor. For example, if a home builder uses cheaper immigrant labor for installing wallboard, he/she will be able to build more houses and therefore will need more skilled carpenters, plumbers, and electricians.

In 2017, the National Academies of Sciences, Engineering, and Medicine published the *Panel on the Economic and Fiscal Consequences of Immigration*, a comprehensive analysis. In the theoretical section on the effect of immigration on wages and employment, they conclude that immigrants change the relative prices of labor and capital, resulting in firms hiring more workers (p. 195). Their main *theoretical* conclusion is that "the arrival of immigrants raises the overall income of the native population that absorbs them: the immigration surplus" (National Academies of Sciences, Engineering, and Medicine, p. 196).

In a summary of empirical studies spanning 20 years, they present data indicating that a 1% increase in the labor supply caused by immigration leads to between a –1.7% to a +0.3% change in wages, primarily affecting black men and high school dropouts (Table 5.2, p. 242). The study concludes that the net effect of immigration on native wages is very small overall (p. 247).[12]

Further, the study emphasizes that immigration is only one (small) factor that influences the U.S. economy. It is difficult to isolate that effect from other factors, especially "production technology, communications technology, and the global economy, which together promote international trade in goods and services (and hence offshoring), global supply chains, and foreign investment" (p. 264).

Another study found that immigrants make the economy more productive, which increases GDP. Called the "immigration surplus," natives experience an increase in income. This has been estimated to be between 0.2% and 0.4% of GDP, between $36 and $72 billion dollars (Orrenius).

## Consumption Effects

There are winners and losers from immigration—some workers face lower wages or are not hired at all. Firms experience lower costs, which can they pass onto consumers in the form of lower prices. As their labor costs fall, firms can increase production, creating more jobs.

The Academy study found, for example, that the willingness of less-skilled immigrants to work at low pay reduced consumption costs—the costs to consumers of goods and services like health care, child care, food preparation, house cleaning, repair, and construction—for millions of Americans. This resulted in "positive net benefits to the U.S. economy during the last two decades of the twentieth century." These low-wage workers simultaneously generated "a redistribution of wealth from low- to high-skilled native-born workers" (NAP, pp. 293–294).

## Government Revenues and Expenditures

Most economists agree that in the short run, there is a cost to immigration in terms of education, medical, and other social services, but that in the long run, there is a net positive fiscal impact. One study found that "the total annual fiscal impact of first-generation adults and their dependents, averaged across 2011–13, is a cost of $57.4 billion, while second and third-plus generation adults create a benefit of $30.5 billion and $223.8 billion, respectively" (Edsall).

With some exceptions, documented immigrants must wait for five years to be eligible for SNAP benefits.[13] "Qualified" immigrants are eligible for TANF (Temporary Assistance for Needy Families), Medicaid, and CHIP (Children's Health Insurance Program) only after they have been in the country for five years (Broder et al.).[14]

One of the largest costs of immigration to the government is public education.[15] In 1982, the U.S. Supreme Court issued *Plyler v. Doe*. In that decision, they held that all children have a constitutional right to a free public education, regardless of immigration status.[16] This decision applies to both documented and undocumented children. Even the dissent acknowledged that it "is senseless for an enlightened society to deprive any children—including [unauthorized immigrants]—of an elementary education," in part because "the long-range costs of excluding any children from the public schools may well outweigh the costs of educating them" (Konings).

Funding for public education, kindergarten to twelfth grade, typically comes primarily from local property taxes. This ruling explains, in part, why the data show that immigrants have a positive effect on the federal budget but a negative effect on state and local budgets.[17] The children of immigrants pay more in taxes than their parents or natives,[18] which raises the question of the wisdom of basing immigration policy on immediate or short-term effects.

Working immigrants, even illegal ones, do pay taxes. Even though undocumented immigrants do not have Social Security Numbers, they are able to file tax returns with an Individual Taxpayer Identification Number (ITIN). In 2015, 4.35 million tax returns were filed using ITINs, accounting for more than $13.6 billion in taxes.[19] Some believe that most of these returns are from undocumented immigrants (Shoichet).

Referring to a 2007 report by the Council of Economic Advisers (CEA), Chairman Edward P. Lazear concluded, "Our review of economic research finds immigrants not only help fuel the Nation's economic growth, but also have an overall positive effect on the income of native-born workers." More recent studies confirm that conclusion.

## Jewish Social Ethics

Abraham was the first immigrant in the Bible. "The Lord said to Abram, 'Go forth from your native land and from your father's house to the land that I will show you'" (Genesis 12:1). The Hebrew word for stranger is *ger*, often used to mean immigrant. *Ahavat Ger*—Loving the stranger—is a basic Jewish value (Schwartz, p. 75). "You shall not oppress a stranger, for you know the feelings of the stranger, having yourselves been strangers in the land of Egypt" (Exodus 23:9). "You shall love the stranger, for you were strangers in the land of Egypt" (Deuteronomy 10:19). No commandment is repeated as often in the Torah as that of protecting the stranger. The rabbis enumerate 36 separate injunctions about strangers (Schwartz, pp. 76–77).

Jews identify with the outsider because they themselves have been outsiders. Starting with the Babylonian exile, 586 BCE, through the twentieth century, Jews faced antisemitism and persecution. And despite their desire to emigrate, Russian *refusniks* were *not* permitted to leave. There has been an upsurge in antisemitic incidents recently, both in the United States and abroad. There were 1879 recorded incidents of antisemitism in the United States in 2018, including the shooting at the synagogue in Pittsburgh in which 11 people died (Anti-Defamation League). And in May 2019, the German antisemitism minister warned Jews not to wear a kippah (skullcap) in public because it was not safe (Robinson).[20]

In post-biblical times, many countries exiled the Jews who lived there (Jewish Virtual Library):

- 1107 Moroccan Almoravid ruler Yoseph Ibn Tashfin orders all Moroccan Jews to convert or leave.
- 1290 King Edward I of England expelled all Jews; they were not permitted to return until 1659.
- 1306–1394 Jews were expelled from northern France.

- March 31, 1492, Queen Isabella and King Ferdinand of Spain expelled the Jews.
- 1496 Jews were expelled from Portugal.

Why is treatment of the stranger (immigrant) an important Jewish value? In the Bible, the *ger* is associated with the widow and the orphan. "[A] weak outsider who needs protection" (Schwartz, p. 77). The biblical commandment to provide for the widow and the orphan is similar to the commandment to provide for the stranger.

A second reason is because Jews are commanded to imitate the ways of God. Throughout the Bible we are told how God deals with the stranger. "God … befriends the stranger, providing him with food and clothing" (Deuteronomy 10:18).

The prophet Malachi phrases this in the strongest possible terms. "But I will step forward to contend against you, and I will act as a relentless accuser against those who have no fear of Me; Who practice sorcery, who commit adultery, who swear falsely, who cheat laborers of their hire, and who subvert [the cause of ] the widow, orphans **and stranger**, said the Lord of Hosts" (Malachi, 3:5, emphasis mine). God considers those who oppress the stranger in the same category as adulterers and those who bear false witness. As one commentator writes, if loving the stranger did not quite make it into the "top 10" commandments, the verse from Malachi seems to be trying to add an amendment. Adultery and false witness are both part of the Ten Commandments, and the prophet is saying that one who does not protect the stranger is no better than one who violates the core covenant from Sinai (Schwartz, p. 78).

And third, because there is a tangible reward. It is almost as if God is not confident in relying on our compassion, so an *incentive* is provided (another example of economic concepts in the Bible).[21] "If you execute justice between one person and another, if you do not oppress the stranger, the orphan and the widow, if you do not shed the blood of an innocent, if you do not follow other Gods … Then will I let you dwell in the land which I gave to our fathers for all time" (Jeremiah 7:5–8).

These biblical passages offer somewhat general directives about the treatment of the stranger. Others are more specific. "There shall be one law for you and for the resident stranger; it shall be a law for all time throughout the ages. You and the stranger are alike before the Lord; the same ritual and the same rule shall apply to you and to the stranger who resides among you" (Numbers 15:15–16).[22]

These biblical passages can be applied directly to one particular public policy issue, college education.[23] The Illegal Immigration Reform and Immigrant Responsibility Act (IIRIRA), passed in 1996, prohibits states from offering in-state tuition rates to undocumented immigrant students, with some exceptions.[24] Currently, 18 states allow in-state tuition for undocumented students (Undocumented State Tuition).

Note that the IIRIRA does not prohibit undocumented students from *attending* public colleges and universities. But requiring them to pay out-of-state tuition (and denying them federal financial aid) is effectively shutting them out of college. State colleges and universities in Pennsylvania charge out-of-state tuition to undocumented students. At Penn State University Park, in-state tuition was $17,416 for first year students for the 2018–19 academic year. The rate for out-of-state students was $33,820, almost double the in-state tuition rate.[25]

Economically, the federal policy is short-sighted. There is consistent evidence that more education leads to higher income. In 2018, median usual weekly earnings were $1198 for workers with a college degree; they were $730 for a worker with a high school diploma.[26] Financial concerns contribute to the higher level of stress and anxiety that undocumented students experience at college over other students (Mulhere).[27]

## Jewish Immigration and Advocacy in the United States

Demographers identify three major waves of Jewish immigration to the United States, all fleeing persecution or worse. The first, 1654–1820, was the smallest. Between 1820 and 1880, almost a quarter of a million Jews came from Europe. The largest migration, 1880–1920, was almost two million Jews, primarily from Europe but also from the Middle East, Asia, and North Africa (Silverman). In the United States, they were greeted with antisemitism and discrimination. Much later, in the 1980s, there was a fourth wave, of Jews from the former Soviet Union.

HIAS (Hebrew Immigration Aid Society) was established to help these immigrants (HIAS). Founded as the Hebrew Immigrant Aid Society in 1881 to assist Jews fleeing pogroms in Russia and eastern Europe, HIAS has touched the life of nearly every Jewish family in America and now welcomes all who have fled persecution. As the need to assist Jewish immigrants diminished, HIAS expanded its work to include anyone in need, regardless of religious affiliation or home country, coming to the United States fleeing persecution of any kind.[28]

In 2005, HIAS crafted the "Interfaith Statement in Support of Comprehensive Immigration Reform," which cites passages from the Bible, the New Testament, and the Qur'an. This statement was a response to pending comprehensive immigration reform legislation in the U.S. Congress and was endorsed by over 35 national organizations, representing a variety of faiths:

> We, the undersigned faith-based leaders and organizations, join together to call upon President (George W.) Bush and our elected officials in Congress to enact comprehensive immigration reform legislation that establishes a safe and humane immigration system consistent with our values. Our diverse faith traditions teach us to welcome our brothers and sisters with love and compassion.[29]

Those attempts to reform the U.S. immigration laws ultimately failed in the Senate, as did proposed legislation for comprehensive immigration reform in 2013 (Valverde).

The Rabbinical Assembly[30] passed a resolution on immigration to the United States in 2007. It cites biblical teachings, the history of Jewish immigration to the United States, the ineffectiveness of current immigration policy, and economic research on the positive effect of immigration:

> You shall not oppress a stranger, for you know the feelings of the stranger (Exodus 23:9)
>
> Whereas the Jewish people have been immigrants and wanders for most of our history;
>
> Whereas the United States, which has long been a home and haven for economic and political refugees, maintained open immigration policies in the early twentieth century that saved the lives of hundreds of thousands of Jews and others; ...[31]

In 2019, over two dozen Jewish organizations signed a document condemning President Trump's "zero-tolerance" policy that leads to family separations:

> Our Jewish faith demands of us concern for the stranger in our midst. Our own people's history as "strangers" reminds us of the many struggles faced by immigrants today and compels our commitment to an immigration system in this country that is compassionate and just.[32]

## Conclusion

From the economics perspective, overall, immigration is good for the economy. "Sharply reducing immigration would be a poorly-targeted and inefficient way to assist low-wage Americans" (U.S. Council of Economic Advisers, p. 641). "Immigration has an overall positive impact on long-run economic growth in the United States" (NASEM).

> Economic analysis finds little support for the view that inflows of foreign labor have reduced jobs or Americans' wages. Economic theory predictions and the bulk of academic research confirms that wages are unaffected by immigration over the long-term, and that the economic effects of immigration are mostly positive for natives and for the overall economy. (Wharton)

The biblical message is unambiguous—act in the imitation of God in the treatment of strangers; there are no conditions or exceptions, because Jews know what it is like to be a stranger. Major Jewish organizations and religious movements have been signatories on resolutions for comprehensive immigration reform based on religious teachings.[33] On the issue of immigration, economics and Jewish social justice lead to the same conclusion: we should welcome immigrants.

In the preface to his book, *Heaven's Door: Immigration Policy and the American Economy*, Harvard economist George Borjas writes, "man cannot live by facts alone. At some point in the debate over social policy, the facts have to be let out of their moral vacuum, the facts have to be interpreted in the context of a set of beliefs, values and a vision of what the U.S. is all about" (p. xiii). In a sense, he seems to embrace the Jewish social justice perspective on immigration.

## Appendix 1: Interfaith Statement in Support of Comprehensive Immigration Reform

October 14, 2005[34]

We, the undersigned faith-based leaders and organizations, join together to call upon President (George W.) Bush and our elected officials in Congress to enact comprehensive immigration reform legislation that establishes a safe and humane immigration system consistent with our values. Our diverse faith traditions teach us to welcome our brothers and sisters with love and compassion.

The Hebrew Bible tells us: "The strangers who sojourn with you shall be to you as the natives among you, and you shall love them as yourself; for you were strangers in the land of Egypt (Leviticus 19:33–34)." In the New Testament, Jesus tells us to welcome the stranger (cf. Matthew 25:35), for "what you do to the least of my brethren, you do unto me (Matthew 25:40)." The Qur'an tells us that we should "serve God … and do good to … orphans, those in need, neighbors who are near, neighbors who are strangers, the companion by your side, the wayfarer that you meet, [and those who have nothing] (4:36)."

We call for immigration reform because each day in our congregations, service programs, health-care facilities, and schools we witness the human consequences of an outmoded system. We see and hear the suffering of immigrant families who have lost loved ones to death in the desert or immigrants themselves who have experienced exploitation in the workplace or abuse at the hands of unscrupulous smugglers and others. In our view, changes to the U.S. legal immigration system would help put an end to this suffering, which offends the dignity of all human beings.

We call upon our elected officials to enact legislation that includes the following:

- An opportunity for hard-working immigrants who are already contributing to this country to come out of the shadows, regularize their status upon satisfaction of reasonable criteria and, over time, pursue an option to become lawful permanent residents and eventually United States citizens;
- Reforms in our family-based immigration system to significantly reduce waiting times for separated families who currently wait many years to be reunited;
- The creation of legal avenues for workers and their families who wish to migrate to the U.S. to enter our country and work in a safe, legal, and orderly manner with their rights fully protected; and
- Border protection policies that are consistent with humanitarian values and with the need to treat all individuals with respect, while

allowing the authorities to carry out the critical task of identifying and preventing entry of terrorists and dangerous criminals, as well as pursuing the legitimate task of implementing American immigration policy.

While we support the right of the government to enforce the law and protect the national security interests of the United States, we recognize that our existing complex and unworkable immigration system has made it nearly impossible for many immigrants—who seek to support their families or reunite with loved ones—to achieve legal status. Reforming the immigration system to address this reality would allow the U.S. government to focus its enforcement efforts on real threats that face all Americans—citizens and immigrants alike.

We urge our elected officials to conduct the immigration reform debate in a civil and respectful manner, mindful not to blame immigrants for our social and economic ills or for the atrocities committed by the few who have carried out acts of terrorism. A polarized process that is lacking in civility would hinder deliberative discourse and not serve the best interests of our nation.

As faith-based leaders and organizations, we call attention to the moral dimensions of public policy and pursue policies that uphold the human dignity of each person, all of whom are made in the image of God. We engage the immigration issue with the goal of fashioning an immigration system that facilitates legal status and family unity in the interest of serving the God-given dignity and rights of every individual. It is our collective prayer that the legislative process will produce a just immigration system of which our nation of immigrants can be proud.

## Appendix 2: Rabbinical Assembly Resolution on Immigration to the United States (2007)[35]

*You shall not oppress a stranger, for you know the feelings of the stranger* (Exodus 23:9)

Whereas the Jewish people have been immigrants and wanderers for most of our history;

Whereas the United States, which has long been a home and haven for economic and political refugees, maintained open immigration policies in the early twentieth century that saved the lives of hundreds of thousands of Jews and others;

Whereas immigrants constitute more than 13% of the United States workforce, yet do not hurt employment opportunities for U.S.-born workers (2006 study by the Pew Hispanic Center);

Whereas an estimated ten to twelve million undocumented immigrants are already living, working, going to school, and paying taxes in the United States; and, in many cases, raising children who are United States citizens;

Whereas the immigrant population pays more in taxes than they collect in public benefits and the Social Security Administration holds $420 billion from the earnings of immigrants who are not qualified to collect social security payments;

Whereas the current immigration system compromises U.S. security by creating a shadow population of millions of undocumented immigrants who are unable to adjust their status; and

Whereas the current enforcement-only approach to immigration has not stemmed the flow of undocumented immigrants, and has led private citizens and local law enforcement authorities, who are not trained in immigration law, to patrol the border and to arrest and detain immigrants.

Thereby be it resolved that the Rabbinical Assembly call upon the United States government to implement an immigration policy that allows the United States to attain its full economic potential;

To create opportunities for earned legalization and a path to citizenship for undocumented immigrants already living in the United States as supported by President George W. Bush and the current U.S. administration;

To prevent the exploitation of immigrant workers by guaranteeing wage and safety protections;

To ensure that those who provide needed supports and services to undocumented immigrants are not criminalized;

To reduce the backlog in the family reunification system to preserve family stability;

To allow immigrants access to public services without fear of retribution; and

To guarantee due process in immigration proceedings and the protection of civil liberties.

## Notes

1. Deferred Action for Childhood Arrivals (Edelman).
2. Trump, Shear.

3. https://budgetmodel.wharton.upenn.edu/issues/2016/1/27/the-effects-of-immigration-on-the-united-states-economy.
4. http://news.gallup.com/poll/1660/immigration.aspx.
5. "Immigrant" is defined as anyone not a U.S. citizen by birth. In these data, no distinction is made between immigrants who are documented and undocumented (MPI, U.S. Immigrant Population and Share over Time, 1850–present).
6. https://www.dhs.gov/immigration-statistics/yearbook/2017/table1 According to DHS, these data are for foreign nationals who are granted lawful permanent residence (i.e., immigrants who receive a "green card"), admitted as temporary nonimmigrants, granted asylum or refugee status, or are naturalized.
7. https://budgetmodel.wharton.upenn.edu/issues/2016/1/27/the-effects-of-immigration-on-the-united-states-economy.
8. I calculated these numbers from data from "Educational Attainment by nativity and region of birth: 1960–2016" referenced in Radford and Budiman. There may be some rounding errors.
9. These numbers were calculated in the same way as the numbers in Note 4.
10. See https://www.migrationpolicy.org/research/timeline-1790 for more information about these laws and a discussion of others.
11. Two of the three senators, Cotton and Perdue, had proposed similar legislation in 2017 that included the proposed test. A version of the test is at http://time.com/4887574/trump-raise-act-immigration/. (Segarra)
12. They do include the caveat that certain "subgroups" may experience a larger, negative impact (p. 247).
13. Exceptions include some refugees and victims of human trafficking. https://www.fns.usda.gov/snap/eligibility/citizen/non-citizen-policy.
14. As with SNAP, there are some exceptions. See Broder et al.
15. Most of the costs of K-12 education come from local real estate taxes.
16. https://www.americanimmigrationcouncil.org/research/plyler-v-doe-public-education-immigrant-students.
17. https://www.nap.edu/resource/23550/RiB-fiscal-immigration.pdf. Note that the effect at the state and local level depends on the number of immigrants.
18. https://www.nap.edu/resource/23550/RiB-fiscal-immigration.pdf.
19. https://www.nbcnews.com/politics/donald-trump/fact-check-how-much-does-illegal-immigration-cost-america-not-n950981.
20. See Walt for a recent analysis of antisemitic incidents in Europe.
21. See Chap. 2 for an analysis of incentives.

22. Note the apparent contradiction with the rules for charging interest. See. Chap. 6.
23. See https://www.nilc.org/issues/education/basic-facts-instate/ for more details about undocumented students and financial aid.
24. Section 505 of the law states "an alien who is not lawfully present in the United States shall not be eligible on the basis of residence within a State (or a political subdivision) for any postsecondary education benefit unless a citizen or national of the United States is eligible for such a benefit (in no less an amount, duration, and scope) without regard to whether the citizen or national is such a resident" (Ali).
25. http://tuition.psu.edu/tuitiondynamic/tabledrivenrates.aspx?location=up.
26. https://www.bls.gov/emp/chart-unemployment-earnings-education.htm.
27. For a moving personal narrative of twin sisters who were students at Notre Dame and undocumented, see "Shattering the Silence: Undocumented Twins Share their Story."
28. Jewish law requires that Jews must care for non-Jews as well as Jews. As Dorff writes, this is based on the Talmud and is "for the sake of peace" (Dorff, p. 130).
29. Interfaith Statement in Support of Comprehensive Immigration Reform October 14, 2005. Complete text is found in Appendix 1 at the end of this chapter.

    https://www.episcopalchurch.org/library/article/interfaith-statement-support-comprehensive-immigration-reform.
30. The organization of rabbis of the Conservative movement.
31. https://jewschool.com/2007/05/12308/comprehensive-immigration-reform-spreads-like-wildfire-we-hope/. Full text of this document can be found in Appendix 2 at the end of this chapter.
32. https://uscj.org/blog/uscj-co-signs-letter-condemning-u-s-zero-tolerance-immigration-policy.
33. https://urj.org/what-we-believe/resolutions/support-comprehensive-immigration-reform-united-states.
34. https://www.episcopalchurch.org/library/article/interfaith-statement-support-comprehensive-immigration-reform.
35. https://jewschool.com/2007/05/12308/comprehensive-immigration-reform-spreads-like-wildfire-we-hope/.

## Bibliography

Ali, Diane. "In-State Tuition for Undocumented Students: 2017 State-Level Analysis." NASPA. July 21, 2017. https://www.naspa.org/rpi/posts/in-state-tuition-for-undocumented-students-2017-state-level-analysis

American Immigration Council. FACT SHEET Public Education for Immigrant Students: Understanding Plyler v. Doe. October 24, 2016. https://www.americanimmigrationcouncil.org/research/plyler-v-doe-public-education-immigrant-students

Anti-Defamation League (ADL). "Anti-Semitic Incidents Remained at Near-Historic Levels in 2018; Assaults Against Jews More Than Doubled". April 30, 2019. https://www.adl.org/news/press-releases/anti-semitic-incidents-remained-at-near-historic-levels-in-2018-assaults

Bolton, Alexander. "GOP senators introduce bill to reduce legal immigration." *The Hill*, April 10, 2019. https://thehill.com/homenews/senate/438221-gop-senators-introduce-bill-to-reduce-legal-immigration

Borjas, George. *Heaven's Door: Immigration Policy and the American Economy.* Princeton, NJ: Princeton University Press, 1999.

Broder, Tanya, Avideh Moussavian, and Jonathan Blazer. "Overview of Immigrant Eligibility for Federal Programs." National Immigration Law Center. December 2015. https://www.nilc.org/issues/economic-support/overview-immeligfedprograms/

Card, David. *Is the New Immigration Really So Bad?* National Bureau of Economic Research Working Paper 11547, August 2006. http://www.nber.org/papers/w11547

Dorff, Elliot. "*The Way into Tikkun Olam (Repairing the World)*. Woodstock, NY: Jewish Lights Publishing, 2005.

Edelman, Adam. "Trump Ends DACA program; No New Applications Accepted." NBC News, September 5, 2017. https://www.nbcnews.com/politics/immigration/trump-dreamers-daca-immigration-announcement-n798686

Edsall, Thomas B. "What Does Immigration Actually Cost Us?" *New York Times*, September 29, 2016. https://www.nytimes.com/2016/09/29/opinion/campaign-stops/what-does-immigration-actually-cost-us.html

Gallop. Immigration. https://news.gallup.com/poll/1660/immigration.aspx

HIAS (Hebrew Immigration Aid Society). https://www.hias.org/

"Interfaith Statement in Support of Comprehensive Immigration Reform." 2005. https://www.episcopalchurch.org/library/article/interfaith-statement-support-comprehensive-immigration-reform

Jones, Bradley. "Majority of Americans continue to say immigrants strengthen the U.S." Pew Research Center *FactTank News in the Numbers*, January 19, 2019. https://www.pewresearch.org/fact-tank/2019/01/31/majority-of-americans-continue-to-say-immigrants-strengthen-the-u-s/

Konings, Priya. "Protecting Immigrant Children's Right to Education." American Bar Association. March 1, 2017. https://www.americanbar.org/groups/child_law/resources/child_law_practiceonline/child_law_practice/vol-36/mar-apr-2017/protecting-immigrant-childrens-right-to-education-/

Jewish Virtual Library. "Timeline of Judaism after the Babylonian Exile (538 BCE–70CE). https://www.jewishvirtuallibrary.org/timeline-of-judaism-after-the-babylonian-exile-538-bce-70-ce

Migration Policy Institute (MPI). "U.S. Immigrant Population and Share over Time, 1850–Present." https://www.migrationpolicy.org/programs/data-hub/us-immigration-trends#history, Number and Share of Total U.S. Population, 1850-2017

Migration Policy Institute (MPI). "Regions of Birth for Immigrants in the United States, 1960-Present." https://www.migrationpolicy.org/programs/data-hub/us-immigration-trends#source, Top Ten Countries of Birth, 1960-2017

Migration Policy Institute (MPI). "Major U.S. Immigration Laws, 1790-Present." Fact Sheets. March 2013. https://www.migrationpolicy.org/research/timeline-1790

Mulhere, Kaitlin. "Undocumented and Stressed." *Inside Higher Ed*. June 26, 2015. https://www.insidehighered.com/news/2015/01/26/study-finds-undocumented-colleges-students-face-unique-challenges

National Academies of Sciences, Engineering, and Medicine (NASEM). *The Economic and Fiscal Consequences of Immigration*. Washington, DC: The National Academies Press, 2017. https://doi.org/10.17226/23550. (Report Highlights. https://www.nap.edu/resource/23550/RiB-fiscal-immigration.pdf)

National Academies of Sciences, Engineering, and Medicine; Division of Behavioral and Social Sciences and Education; Committee on National Statistics; Panel on the Economic and Fiscal Consequences of Immigration; Francine D. Blau and Christopher Mackie, Editors. https://www.nap.edu/catalog/23550/the-economic-and-fiscal-consequences-of-immigration

Orrenius, Pia. "Benefits of Immigration Outweigh the Costs." *The Catalyst, A Journal of Ideas from the Bush Institute*. Issue 02. Spring 2016. https://www.bushcenter.org/catalyst/north-american-century/benefits-of-immigration-outweigh-costs.html

Radford, Jynnah and Abby Budiman. "Facts of U.S. Immigration, 2016." Pew Research Center, September 14, 2018. https://www.pewhispanic.org/2018/09/14/facts-on-u-s-immigrants/

Roberts, Nina. "Undocumented immigrants quietly pay billions into Social Security and receive no benefits." *Marketplace*, January 28, 2019. https://www.marketplace.org/2019/01/28/undocumented-immigrants-quietly-pay-billions-social-security-and-receive-no/

Schwartz, Rabbi Sidney. *Judaism and Justice: The Jewish Passion to Repair the World*. Woodstock, Vermont: Jewish Lights Publishing, 2006.

Segarra, Aria and David Johnson, "Find Out if President Trump Would Let You Immigrate to America." *Time Magazine*. August 7, 2017. http://time.com/4887574/trump-raise-act-immigration/

Shattering the Silence: Undocumented Twins Share their Story. University of Notre Dame, 2015. https://www.nd.edu/stories//shattering-the-silence/

Shear, Michael D. "Trump Immigration Proposal Emphasizes Immigrants' Skills Over Family Ties." *New York Times*, May 15, 2019. https://www.nytimes.com/2019/05/15/us/politics/trump-immigration-kushner.html

Shoichet, Catherine E. "Undocumented immigrants are paying their taxes today, too." CNN, April 15, 2019. https://www.cnn.com/2019/04/15/us/taxes-undocumented-immigrants/index.html

Silverman, Dara. "And If Not Together, How?: Jews and Immigration to the United States." In *Righteous Indignation: A Jewish Call for Justice*. Or N. Rose, Margie Klein, and Jo Ellen Green Kaiser, editors. Jewish Lights Publishing, 2009, pp. 163–168.

SNAP Policy on Non-Citizen Eligibility. https://www.fns.usda.gov/snap/eligibility/citizen/non-citizen-policy

*Tanahk: A New Translation of the Holy Scriptures*. Philadelphia, The Jewish Publication Society, 1985.

Trump, Donald J. "Remarks by President Trump on Modernizing Our Immigration System for a Stronger America." May 16, 2019. https://www.whitehouse.gov/briefings-statements/remarks-president-trump-modernizing-immigration-system-stronger-america/

"Undocumented Student Tuition: Overview." National Conference of State Legislatures (NCSL), March 14, 2019. http://www.ncsl.org/research/education/undocumented-student-tuition-overview.aspx

Union of Reform Judaism. "Support of Comprehensive Immigration Reform in the United States." 2007. https://urj.org/what-we-believe/resolutions/support-comprehensive-immigration-reform-united-states

United States Department of Labor, Bureau of Labor Statistics. Economics News Release. May 16, 2019. Table 1. Employment status of the foreign-born and native-born populations by selected characteristics, 2017–2018 annual averages. https://www.bls.gov/news.release/forbrn.t01.htm

United States Department of Labor, Bureau of Labor Statistics. Economics News Release. May 16, 2019. Table 4. Employed foreign-born and native-born persons 16 years and over by occupation and sex, 2018 annual averages. https://www.bls.gov/news.release/forbrn.t04.htm

United States Department of Labor, Bureau of Labor Statistics. Economics News Release. May 16, 2019 Table 5. Median usual weekly earnings of full-time wage and salary workers for the foreign born and native born by selected characteristics, 2017–2018 annual averages. https://www.bls.gov/news.release/forbrn.t05.htm

"The US Council of Economic Advisers on Immigration's Economic Impact." *Population and Development Review*, vol. 33, no. 3, 2007, pp. 641–646. JSTOR, www.jstor.org/stable/25434649

Valverde, Miriam. "Did Senate pass immigration bills in 2006, 2013 and House failed to vote on them?" *Punditfact*, January 26, 2018. https://www.politifact.com/punditfact/statements/2018/jan/26/ronald-brownstein/did-senators-pass-immigration-reform-bills-2006-20/

Walt, Vivienne. "Europe's Jews Are Resisting a Rising Tide of Anti-Semitism." *Time*. June 20, 2019. https://time.com/longform/anti-semitism-in-europe/

CHAPTER 5

# Climate

**Abstract** Environmental issues are examples of negative externalities, which occur when a person's or firm's actions have unintended effects on others. They can be remedied by taxes or government regulation. Over 3500 economists endorsed a carbon tax as the best way to deal with climate change.

Jewish teaching emphasizes avoiding harm. There is no such concept as an acceptable level of environmental damage. But there is ambiguity on this—if an action that results in harm to others, as is the case of polluting a stream, is necessary for someone's livelihood, it is permitted. But in most cases, the good of the community always takes precedence over the individual, a direct contrast to market economics.

**Keywords** Externalities • Carbon tax • Community

*"And everything I made, I created for you. Be careful [though], that you don't spoil or destroy My world—because if you spoil it, there's nobody after you to fix it."*
Kohelet Rabbah 7:13



N. R. Fox, *Profits and Prophets*,
https://doi.org/10.1007/978-3-030-40556-4_5

## Introduction

Although economists, politicians, and scientists have only relatively recently seriously considered environmental problems, Jewish law has been addressing them for thousands of years. In this chapter, I analyze the theory of environmental economics and recommended policies to address climate change. I then discuss Jewish teaching on the environment and possible implications for current environmental policies. On this topic, there is a deep divide between the market and Jewish social justice tradition perspectives. Economists analyze the costs and benefits of environmental problems to determine the optimal, or efficient, level, which is a usually positive number. Traditional Jewish teaching says there cannot be an acceptable level of harm to the community, privileging the common good over the individual, with only a few, notable exceptions.

## Economic Analysis

As discussed in Chap. 2, the market results in an efficient outcome only under certain conditions.[1] If these conditions are not satisfied, the result is termed a market failure. Externalities are one type of market failure and occur when one person's or firm's actions have unintended, sometimes called spillover, effects on someone else. This occurs when the social costs of an activity are not included in decision making. Smoking is an excellent example.

Presumably, a rational person makes the decision to smoke by weighing the costs and benefits of a decision. Costs include the actual money spent on the purchase as well as health effects. Benefits might include keeping off excess weight and fitting in with friends. Because an individual is deemed to know their preferences best, in a perfectly functioning market, these preferences would not be questioned (assuming that the individual has complete and accurate information), and this would be considered an efficient outcome. But because this person's decision to smoke has negative, unintended effects on others, this is an example of a negative externality, and the decision to smoke is inefficient.[2] Second- (and third-) hand smoke affects people in proximity of smokers, and smokers do not take this effect into account when deciding to smoke. They therefore smoke more than is socially optimal.

To understand the distinction between private and social costs, consider a paper mill. It uses many inputs—electricity, wood pulp, labor—and it pays for all of these inputs. But the production of paper results in emissions into the air, including methanol, acetaldehyde, formaldehyde, and other hazardous air pollutants (United States Environmental Protection Agency). The air is free, so the mill does not have to pay for using it, even though it is an input into production as much as the wood pulp is. Because the mill does not take the social cost into account as it calculates the profit maximizing amount of paper to produce (with necessarily accompanying emissions), it will produce more than is efficient. When firms maximize profit, they are minimizing cost. Because they do not have to account for all of the costs, they overproduce.

This concept is closely related to the idea of private property. A firm cannot use electricity, workers, or wood pulp unless it pays for them from the producers. Because the air is not owned by anyone, because it is not private property, anyone can use it, which is the source of the negative externality.[3]

Producers succeed in the market when they produce what consumers want at the lowest cost. When the firm does not have to pay for some of the resources, as is the case with negative externalities, it overuses them and understates the cost of production. That is the reason for the inefficient level of production.[4]

### *The Coase Theorem*

In 1991, Ronald Coase won the Nobel Prize for his work on externalities.[5] The Coase Theorem states that under certain circumstances, the market can achieve an efficient level of an activity even if there are externalities. Consider this example.[6] Suppose a factory creates noise that bothers someone living nearby. The factory can muffle the noise with equipment that costs $1000; the neighbor can pay $1500 to insulate her home. She pays the factory $1000 to install the noise muffling equipment. She is better off by $500 and has less noise. The factory is better off by $1000, and the optimal amount of noise is produced without the need for government intervention. "Even if the factory owner is not forced to fix the problem, it will pay the homeowner to bribe the factory owner to reduce the noise via the low-cost remedy" (Baumol and Blinder, p 308). We do not observe this result more frequently because of transaction costs—the costs of making the deal. These include costs of communication and the cost of enforcement.

But a Coase result did occur in New York City. In 2016, residents of an apartment building in the Chelsea neighborhood of Manhattan were concerned about losing their view to a new building that was planned adjacent to theirs. They offered the developer $11 million *not to build the condominium*, and he accepted (people living on lower floors paid less than those living on higher floors) (Goodman).

## Government Remedies

When the market results in inefficient levels of an activity because of externalities, government intervention is required to correct the situation. Though most economists agree on the general concept, there are differences about the type of action the government should take and how severe the problem has to be to warrant action at all. Generally, the government has two options: it can regulate by setting requirements that must be met or it can tax, which internalizes the external cost.

### *Pigouvian Taxes*

"[T]he most effective way to attack climate change: [is] using taxes and market forces rather than government controls to reduce harmful emissions" (Rattner). For proponents of the market, the best outcome results from market interactions. If externalities result in an inefficient outcome, then the preferred solution is to internalize the externalities. This typically means assessing a tax that will force firms (or individuals) to pay for all of the resources they are using in production so that the private costs include the social costs. This type of tax is usually called a Pigouvian tax, after economist Arthur Pigou.[7]

In 2018, over 3000 economists, including all 4 (living) former chairs of the Federal Reserve Board, 15 former chairs of the Council of Economic Advisers, and 27 Nobel Laureates, endorsed a carbon tax as the best way to deal with climate change.[8] It is noteworthy that among the Federal Reserve chairs and former chairs of the Council of Economic Advisors, half were appointed by Republican presidents and half by Democratic presidents. It is significant to find so much agreement on this policy in a profession that is notorious for rarely being on the same page. "A carbon tax offers the most cost-effective lever to reduce carbon emissions at the scale and speed that is necessary. By correcting a well-known market failure, a carbon tax will send a powerful price signal that harnesses the invisible hand of the marketplace to steer economic actors towards a low-carbon future."[9]

The statement recommends increasing the tax until emissions goals are met and argues that this system will be superior in many ways to government regulation. Raising the price of these fuels would create an incentive for industry to find cheaper alternatives (Rattner), which is precisely one of the functions of price in a market—it directs resources to the lowest cost alternatives. Results from a 2018 poll conducted by the Energy Policy Institute at the University of Chicago and the AP-NORC Center indicate that of those who believe climate change is real, 47% support a tax on carbon-based fuels. And 57% of them are willing to pay a $1 monthly fee; 23% are willing to pay a monthly fee of $40 (AP).

The statement also addresses the possible issue of American firms' competitiveness abroad.[10] Perhaps its most creative contribution is its proposal for what to do with the revenues that are collected. Typically, tax revenue is used to support government programs. Some tax revenue is targeted for particular projects; other revenues are general funds. Their proposal recommends returning the revenue directly to American families via a lump sum payment in order to "maximize the fairness and political viability of a rising carbon tax."[11] This proposal is similar to a law recently enacted in Canada.

In 2018, Canada passed the Greenhouse Gas Pollution Pricing Act, which imposed a $20 per ton tax on emissions in 2019, gradually increasing until it reaches $50 per ton in 2022. Revenues from the tax will be returned to the provinces, which will distribute all but 10% to their residents. The tax not only is designed to be revenue neutral but is also expected to compensate Canadians for about 70% of the expected increase in energy costs (Nuccitelli).

In addition to discouraging or penalizing actions with a tax, the government can also encourage behavior with a subsidy, which is the opposite of a tax. It is a financial reward for taking a particular action. In order to encourage more people to buy electric automobiles, the U.S. government offered a tax credit to buyers, effectively lowering the purchase price of the vehicle.[12] Beginning in 2010, consumers who purchased a hybrid or all-electric vehicle were eligible for a tax credit of up to $7500. The amount will be reduced through 2020.[13]

An alternative to tax is for the government to require or prohibit some sort of action. Individuals have no choice; if they fail to comply, they face a penalty. As an example, in 2012 President Obama announced that all cars and light trucks produced in the United States would be required to achieve a fuel economy of 54.5 MPG by model year 2025. The regulation was implemented to achieve numerous goals, including reduced dependence on foreign oil, reduced carbon emissions, and addressing climate change. Major automakers endorsed the standards which were expected to "cut greenhouse gas emissions from cars and light trucks in half by 2025, reducing emissions by 6 billion metric tons over the life of the program—more than the total amount of carbon dioxide emitted by the United States in 2010" (The White House). Despite the expected higher cost of the vehicles, consumers are expected to save money in the long run because of lower fuel costs. Six years later, under President Trump, those standards were rolled back to 37 (Cama and Green).

### *Cap and Trade*

Cap and trade can be considered a blend of government regulation and a market solution. Under this system, the government issues licenses that allow a certain amount of pollutants that can be emitted. Firms are then permitted to trade those permits among themselves. A market emerges, establishing a price for the permits. In this case, the total amount of emissions is set, but it doesn't matter (to the government) where they are coming from. The result is a decrease in pollution at minimum cost.

For example, suppose that it will cost Firm A $200 to reduce emissions and Firm B $500, because it has older technology. Firm B could purchase a permit to pollute from Firm A for $300. Firm A gives up its permission to pollute in exchange for $300. Because it costs Firm A $200 to curb emissions, Firm A is better off by $100. Firm B has paid $300 for the right to pollute, saving $200 from the cost of polluting. Both firms are better off, which is expected in voluntary market exchange, and there are fewer pollutants released into the air.

The 1990 amendment to the Clean Air Act of 1970 established this type of system for sulfur dioxide, a pollutant in acid rain (McCarthy and Copeland, p. 10). The program was an overwhelming success. From 1990 to 2018, the national average of sulfur dioxide emissions declined by 89%.[14]

### *The State of the Climate*

In 2018, two influential studies about climate change were released. The United Nation's Intergovernmental Panel on Climate Change (IPPC) studies the impact of global warming under the assumption of a 1.5 °C increase in temperature and greenhouse gas emissions. The report emphasized that global warming is caused by human activities and that oceans, wildlife, and agriculture are among the areas that will be affected if drastic steps are not taken soon to address climate change (International Panel on Climate Change, IPPC). The report recommends a carbon tax to reduce emissions (Davenport and Pierre-Louis).

Shortly after the U.N. report was released, Yale economist William D. Nordhaus was awarded the 2018 Nobel Memorial Prize in Economic Sciences in recognition of his decades of work on the economics of climate change.[15] He created a quantitative model "that describes the global interplay between the economy and the climate. His model integrates theories and empirical results from physics, chemistry and economics. Nordhaus' model is now widely spread and is used to simulate how the economy and the climate co-evolve. It is used to examine the consequences of climate policy interventions, for example carbon taxes" (Nobel Prize). "'There is basically no alternative to the market solution,' Professor Nordhaus said" (Appelbaum).

The Global Change Research Act of 1990 mandates that the U.S. Global Change Research Program (USGCRP) delivers a report to Congress and the President at last every four years (Fourth National Climate Assessment, NCA4) that analyzes the effects of global change on "the natural environment, agriculture, energy production and use, land and water resources, transportation, human health and welfare, human social systems, and biological diversity" and predicts trends for up to 100 years (NCA4). In November 2018, the Fourth National Climate assessment was released.[16]

The report stresses in the strongest possible terms that climate change is a threat to "human health and safety, quality of life, and the rate of economic growth" (NCA4). The report addresses environmental issues in 12 areas, including oceans, water, forests, agriculture, and transportation. Regarding economic effects, it states, "Without substantial and sustained global mitigation and regional adaptation efforts, climate change is expected to cause growing losses to American infrastructure and property and impede the rate of economic growth over this century" (NCA4). It predicts losses of hundreds of billions of dollars by the end of the century if emissions continue to grow. And even though there have been some improvements since the last report in 2014, "more immediate and substantial global greenhouse gas emissions reductions, as well as regional adaptation efforts, would be needed to avoid the most severe consequences in the long term" (NCA4).

## Jewish Social Justice

### *Introduction: Stewardship and Care for the Earth*

In 1967, Lynn White published an influential article in *Science* that basically attributed environmental problems to religion (White). This claim was widely disputed by scholars of religion for its narrow interpretation of the so-called Dominion Mandate, based on Genesis 1: 26–28. "They (man) shall rule ... the whole earth ... fill the earth and master it."

The Jewish teachings on climate emphasize stewardship because the earth does not belong to people; it belongs to God. "For the land is mine" (Leviticus, 25:23). "That you may know that the earth is the Lord's" (Exodus 9:29). There is an understanding that people have an obligation to take care of the earth and to avoid destroying it. This interpretation comes from two sources. "Everything I have created; I have created for you. *Be mindful that you do not ruin and devastate my world ...*" (*Kohelet Rabbah* 7:13) (Waskow, p. 93). Adam is placed in Eden "to work and *protect it*" (Genesis 2:15).

The critical biblical concept to which most environmental laws and regulations are traced is *Bal Tashchit*, translated as "you shall not wantonly destroy" (Helfand, p. 133). Wasting natural resources is forbidden (Lamm, p. 87). Most of the law concerning the environment derives from this biblical verse (Helfand, p. 133). "When in war against a city you have to besiege it a long time in order to capture it, you must not destroy its trees, wielding the ax against them. You may eat of them, but you must not cut them down" (Deuteronomy 20:19).

If even the extreme situation of wartime is not sufficient reason to make an exception to *Bal Tashchit*, then "how much more so regarding day to day situations of personal comfort and economic profit and loss?" (Bernstein, p. 98). This verse has been interpreted to include other natural resources; "in our day, the inefficient use of fuel would be considered a transgression" (Tamari, p. 285).

### *Externalities*

A recognition of the concept of negative externalities appears early and explicitly in Jewish texts. There is a very strong, consistent teaching, repeated in many sources, that the person causing damages is liable for their negative effects, regardless of whether or not they are caused intentionally. These rules apply to both damages caused to an individual and damages affecting the wider community. It is less clear whether financial compensation, as one might expect an economist to propose, is acceptable in any circumstances. "It is prohibited to introduce pollutants to public water sources" (*Tosefta Bava Metzia* 11:31) *or to allow one's private septic system to leach into a neighbor's well* (*Shulchan Arukh, Choshe Mishpat* 155:21) (Reisner, p. 19).

This responsibility for damages is not limited to direct effects. "Even activities initiated on my property that spread and do damage elsewhere—a fire that gets out of control, an animal that gets away—are my complete responsibility" (Bernstein, 128). The biblical source of these rulings is found in Exodus. "When a man opens a pit, or digs a pit and does not cover it, and an ox or an ass falls into it, the one responsibility of the pit must pay restitution" (Exodus. 21:33). "When a fire is started and spreads to thorns, so that stacked, standing, or growing grain is consumed, he who started the fire must make restitution" (Exodus 22:5).

These rulings clearly convey the concept of negative externalities—one person's actions may have an effect on others—and that they are responsible for any damages that are caused (Dobb, p. 171). Rules prohibit keeping garbage, operating kilns, keeping carcasses or tanneries within city limits because of the negative effects on the air (Reisner, p 19).

A rabbinic story, which seems as if it could be *verbatim* from current economic literature, illustrates the concept of externalities. "This is like people that were sitting on a boat. One of them took a drill and began to drill under his own place. His fellow travelers said to him, 'What are you doing?' He said, 'What do you care—aren't I drilling [only] under my own place?' They said, 'The water will rise and cover us all'" (Dobb, p. 171).

### *Limits to the Market and Market Remedies*

There is broad consensus in Jewish teaching that people should not engage in practices that adversely affect others (and themselves as well). "Pollution must be prevented; once it settles in, it cannot be remedied by religious action or petition" (Frymer-Kensky, p. 68). There is a wider range of opinion and interpretation concerning whether monetary compensation is an acceptable solution. Tamari (p. 280) states that payment is never acceptable, even if the damaged party can be made better off financially.

It should not be surprising that concern for community is an important concept in Jewish teaching on the environment. As Tamari writes, "in this area of environmental welfare, this is a perpetual struggle between unbridled individual freedom to do with … one's property whatever one would like, and the common good" (p. 281). Damage to the public is considered to be akin to robbery (Bernstein, p. 129). Rabbinic texts stress that communal concerns—climate, public health, safety, among others—are more important than "'private property rights' or even 'economic growth' … *the Rabbis insisted that private gains cannot overshadow the public good*" ([emphasis mine] Dobb, p. 171).

Behavior that has adverse environmental effects is prohibited. Unlike other prohibited activities, there are no penalties explicitly stated for forbidden behavior. Typically, penalties are determined in a court (Cardin, p. 3). The absolute prohibition of such activities is an implicit recognition of limits to the market—some things should not be determined in the marketplace because they are based on non-economic values. The purpose of the law is prevention, and the purpose of being knowledgeable about the laws is to avoid the prescribed behavior. This is completely the opposite of cost-benefit decision making.

For example, it is illegal to park in a handicapped parking space if you do not have a decal. Most would agree this is a good and moral rule. Most people obey it. But some might engage in cost-benefit analysis. Some will conclude the benefit (presumably a parking space closer to their destination) is not worth the cost. Others will park there illegally knowing that they might face a fine of up to $200. The purpose of the fine, as an economist would see it, is to provide a disincentive for those without a decal to park in a handicapped space. Because the parking space is essentially available for a price (the fine), the market determines who will park there, not the regulator.

The prohibition of these types of actions signals "the rabbis' willingness to contain a certain amount of individual autonomy in the name of the greater good." They recognized that there is a conflict between individual property rights and the common good (Tamari, p. 281). These teachings support the concept of government regulation over market remedies to environmental damage. In the case of health-related damages, the prohibition is absolute (Tamari, p. 294).

This supports the case for government regulation, instead of market remediation, because there is a moral imperative not to pollute. "A man is not permitted to do damage on the assumption that he will be able to pay for what he has caused, since it is forbidden to cause damage" (*Mishneh Torah Hilkhot Nizkei Mamon Ch 5 halakha 1*) (Tamari, p. 282).[17]

Even when the party who is damaged is willing to accept financial compensation, such transactions are prohibited in the case of pollution. The "law specifies that while some damages may be waived consensually, pollution damages may not be waived" (*SA Chosen Mishpat* 155:36). "[O]ne is not permitted to cause damage, planning to pay damage. Even to cause the damage is prohibited. *[Hilkhot Nizkei Mamon 5:1]*" (Reisner, p.20).

Despite what seems to be strong and unambiguous statements regarding the prohibition of financial compensation for damages, there is an awareness that this type of transaction could be an option. It is as if we were reading an economics text about the Coase Theorem:

> the injured party sometimes has the option of accepting the presence of damages or environmental obstacles in return for payment. He is able to sell some of his rights, as it were, to the party causing the damage. *The halakhah recognizes the possibility that it may be cheaper for the one causing the damage to pay damages than to involve himself in the cost of removing the obstacle altogether or operating his business in such a way as to reduce noise or pollution or other forms of damage* [my emphasis]. The majority opinions in the rabbinic sources see the provision of monetary compensation as secondary, compared with the moral injunction of not causing the damages. (Tamari, p. 283)

Recognizing that some activities cannot be avoided and do not have substitutes, the rabbis allow some exceptions to this prohibition, illustrating the rabbis' willingness to acknowledge the reality of every day economic life. Similarly, if an entire community's financial well-being would suffer, the offending practice may continue (unless the damage is health-related) (Tamari, p. 296). Activities that are necessary to earn a living, even if they cause damage, are permitted (Tamari, p. 288).

> 'It [preventing damages to others] does not apply to the smoke created by the normal activity of a household. Were this to be the case, nobody would be able to build a house and make a fire beneath his food' (*T'shuvot HaRashba, part 2, section 65*). ... there exists a concept of damage caused by the normal activities of people, without which it would not be possible to continue any kind of human activity. In such a case, the property rights of other individuals would have to be abrogated. (Tamari, p. 286)

Economists would object to this type of exception in favor of a market solution. When activities adversely affect others and are permitted to continue, there is no incentive for the offending party to seek an alternative. If the activities are prohibited or if there is a price, then people will be forced to find an alternative, one that presumably causes less damage.

Consider the case of automobiles. We could eliminate traffic deaths and pollution from cars by banning them. But if we did that, we would lose not only the costs of cars but also the benefits. By taxing gasoline or regulating fuel efficiency, we are providing an incentive (or mandating the behavior) to create more fuel-efficient vehicles. If we allowed an exception to driving a gas guzzler for people who need to drive to work, the damage would continue.

### *Long-Run Effects*

As Paul Gorman (National Religious Partnership for the environment) said, "Global warming isn't about carbon emissions; it's about intergeneration equity" (Bernstein, p. 137). Many Jewish texts admonish us to be aware of the long-term implications of environmental damages because some damage is irreparable and because each generation is responsible for the next. There is some damage that is irreparable. There is an emphasis that this generation is responsible for the next. Even where there are important short-run benefits, if there is long-term damage, the activity is prohibited (Bernstein, p. 94).

"[H]as been given to them for all generations, no generation is permitted to change it as it sees fit ... *And each (generation) is required to bequeath it to future generations in the same state in which they received it*" (Bernstein p. 137, emphasis mine). Jewish texts support this concept. "Choose life, so that you *and your children* may live" (Deuteronomy 10:19, emphasis mine). "If you ruin it, there is no one to come after you to put it right" (Kohelet Rabbah 7:13, Bernstein, p. 22).

One of the most well-known stories illustrates this awareness of the responsibility for the long run. "One day Honi was walking down the road, and he sees a man planting a carob tree. Honi said to him: 'Since the carob doesn't bear fruit for 70 years, are you so sure that you'll live 70 years and eat from it?' The man replied: 'I found a world that was full of carob trees. Just like my ancestors planted for me, so I plant for my descendants'" (Dobb, p. 167).

## Conclusion

The economics of climate change is unambiguous. Environmental damage results from negative externalities, a situation where a person or firm does not incur the full cost of their actions, which have negative effects on others. As an example of market failure, externalities are a situation that calls for government intervention to achieve an efficient solution. Government may either regulate—create rules that individuals and firms must follow—or tax, which internalizes the externality, forcing the firm or individual to pay for all the costs of the activity. When costs increase, production of a good or service decreases, which is the desired result.

While rarely in agreement as a profession, most economists favor the market solution of a tax, especially on carbon emissions. Recently over 3000 economists signed a proposal endorsing this policy, and William D. Nordhaus was awarded the 2018 Nobel Prize in Economics for his decades of work on the topic. Recent reports released by the U.S. Global Change Research Program and the United Nations paint a dire picture of the future unless immediate and drastic steps are taken to curb emissions.

In the Jewish tradition, the earth belongs to God, and people are required to care for it. Though the economic term is not used, there is an early and frequent recognition of the concept of externalities in Jewish texts. They state that when someone causes damage to someone else (or to society) they are responsible for the problem. Whenever possible, such behavior should be prevented, with an emphasis on the common good over private property. While the possibility of compensation for such behavior is considered, it is to be discouraged.

## Appendix: Advocacy

Jewish organizations have been active in advocating for the environment. In 2015, The Shalom Center, under the leadership of Rabbi Arthur Waskow, issued a rabbinic letter on the climate crisis environment, inviting clergy and congregants to sign. The document invokes Jewish teaching and cites examples of urgent environmental concerns.

> So we call for a new sense of eco-social justice—a tikkun olam that includes tikkun tevel, the healing of our planet. We urge those who have been focusing on social justice to address the climate crisis, and those who have been focusing on the climate crisis to address social justice.

> Though as rabbis we are drawing on the specific practices by which our Torah makes eco-social justice possible, we recognize that in all cultures and all spiritual traditions there are teachings about the need for setting time and space aside for celebration, restfulness, reflection.[18]

Both the Rabbinical Assembly of the Conservative movement and the Religious Action Center (RAC) of the Reform movement have been active in calling on their own congregations to institute sustainable practices in their synagogues (Halpert).

"We cannot accept the escalating destruction of our environment and its effect on human health and livelihood. It is our sacred duty to alleviate environmental degradation and the human suffering it causes instead of despoiling our air, land, and water. In 2009, the Religious Action Center passed a resolution on climate change."[19] In 2017, the RAC passed the "Resolution on Addressing the Impacts of Climate Change."

1. Encourage congregations to advocate from the local to federal levels of government to uphold or go beyond the commitments of the Paris Climate Agreement;
2. Encourage congregations to:
    a. Take steps to educate and prepare themselves and their neighbors for the impacts of sea level rise, wildfires, increased extreme weather events, drought, and other impacts of climate change; and
    b. Work with local organizations to provide relief to those affected by these events.
3. Continue to advocate for legislative, regulatory, and judicial action to protect all communities from the damaging impacts of climate change;
4. Continue to advocate for the Canadian and U.S. governments to uphold our international responsibilities to decrease the human impacts of climate change; and
5. Encourage congregations to work with interfaith and other partners within their communities to advocate for and work to implement climate change solutions.[20]

The Coalition on the Environment and Jewish Life (COEJL) was established in 1992. Its 29 participants engage in both advocacy and education. According to its mission statement,

"The Coalition on the Environment and Jewish Life engages Jewish institutions and individuals in bringing the moral passion of Jewish tradition and social action to environmental stewardship in order to preserve the integrity of creation, advance social justice, protect future generations, and strengthen the Jewish community." (http://www.coejl.net/about.html)

## Notes

1. See Chap. 2, pp. 25–26.
2. There are also positive externalities when an individual's decision has a positive effect on others that the individual does not take into account. Getting vaccinated is a good example. A vaccination protects me from getting sick, and if I am not sick, then I cannot pass the illness to someone else. Because the economic analysis of environmental policy is based on negative externalities, I will not include further discussion of positive externalities here.
3. See Baumol and Blinder, Chapter 16, for a more extensive discussion.
4. See Baumol and Blinder, p. 305, for a more detailed discussion.
5. https://www.nobelprize.org/prizes/economic-sciences/1991/coase/facts/.
6. See Baumol and Blinder, p. 308, for a full explanation.
7. Pigou wrote in the early twentieth century, before the Nobel Prize was established.
8. For the complete (very brief) five-point statement, see "Economists' Statement" at https://www.clcouncil.org/economists-statement/.
9. https://www.clcouncil.org/economists-statement/.
10. https://www.clcouncil.org/economists-statement/.
11. https://www.clcouncil.org/economists-statement/.
12. https://www.energy.gov/eere/electricvehicles/electric-vehicles-tax-credits-and-other-incentives
13. https://www.fueleconomy.gov/feg/taxevb.shtml.
14. Enacted in 1990, the cap and trade program went into effect in 1994. https://www.epa.gov/air-trends/sulfur-dioxide-trends.
15. The Nobel Prize in Economics is different from other Nobel Prizes. It was established in 1968 by the Sveriges Riksbank (Sweden's central bank) and is technically called the Prize in Economic Sciences in Memory of Alfred Nobel, founder of the Nobel Prize. https://www.nobelprize.org/prizes/economic-sciences/.
16. See https://nca2018.globalchange.gov/chapter/front-matter-about/ for the full text of the mandate.

17. Tamari (p. 282) points out that the rabbis recognized what is essentially the outcome of the Coase Theorem but that the moral imperative of avoiding the proscribed behavior takes precedence.
18. See https://theshalomcenter.org/civicrm/petition/sign?sid=17 for the complete text of the document, "A Rabbinic Letter."
19. https://rac.org/position-reform-movement-environment.
20. https://urj.org/what-we-believe/resolutions/resolution-addressing-impacts-climate-change.

## Bibliography


Appelbaum, Binyamin. "2018 Nobel in Economics Is Awarded to William Nordhaus and Paul Romer." *New York Times*, October 8, 2018. https://www.nytimes.com/2018/10/08/business/economic-science-nobel-prize.html?module=inline.

AP-NORC. "Is the Public Willing to Help Fix Climate Change?" http://www.apnorc.org/projects/Pages/Is-the-Public-Willing-to-Pay-to-Help-Fix-Climate-Change-.aspx

Baumol, William J. and Alan S. Blinder. *Microeconomics: Principles and Policy*, Thirteenth Edition. Boston: Cengage Learning, 2016.

Bernstein, Jeremy. *The Way into Judaism and the Environment*. Woodstock, VT: Jewish Lights Publishing, 2006.

Cama, Timothy and Miranda Green. "Trump moves to roll back Obama emission standards." *The Hill*. August 02, 2018. https://thehill.com/policy/energy-environment/400036-trump-submits-rule-to-weaken-iconic-obama-car-efficiency-standards.

Cardin, Rabbi Nina Beth. "Neighbors and Neighborly Relations." in *The Observant Life*.

Davenport, Coral and Kendra Pierre-Louis. "U.S. Climate Report Warns of Damaged Environment and Shrinking Economy." *New York Times*, November 23, 2018. https://www.nytimes.com/2018/11/23/climate/us-climate-report.html.

Dobb, Fred. "The Rabbis and Expanding Environmental Consciousness" in Waskow, *Torah of the Earth*, pp. 157–178.

"Economists' Statement on Carbon Dividends: The Largest Public Statement of Economists in History." https://www.clcouncil.org/economists-statement/.

Fourth National Climate Assessment (NCA4). https://nca2018.globalchange.gov/.

Frymer-Kensky, Tivka. "Ecology in a Biblical Perspective." in Waskow, *Torah of the Earth*, pp. 55–68.

Goodman, J. David. "How Much Is a View Worth in Manhattan? Try $11 Million." *New York Times*, July 22, 2019. https://www.nytimes.com/2019/07/22/nyregion/manhattan-real-estate-views-air-rights.html.

Halpert, Julie. "Judaism and Climate Change." *The Yale Forum on Climate Change and the Media*. February 29, 2012. http://www.yaleclimatemediaforum.org/2012/02/judaism-and-climate-change/.

Helfand, Jonathan. "The Earth is the Lord's: Judaism and Environmental Ethics." In Waskow, *Torah of the Earth*, pp. 141–156.

International Panel on Climate Change (IPPC). *Special Report: Global Warming of 1.5 degrees C—Summary for Policy Makers*. October 2018. https://www.ipcc.ch/sr15/chapter/spm/.

Lamm, Norman. "Ecology in Jewish Law." in Waskow, *Torah of the Earth*, pp. 103–126.

McCarthy, James E. and Claudia Copeland. *Clean Air Act: A Summary of the Act and Its Major Requirements*. Congressional Research Service, January 11, 2013. https://www.lankford.senate.gov/imo/media/doc/Clean%20Air%20Act%20A%20Summary%20of%20the%20Act%20and%20Its%20Major%20Requirements.pdf.

Nobel Prize. "Press Release: The Prize in Economic Sciences 2018." October 8, 2018. https://www.nobelprize.org/prizes/economic-sciences/2018/press-release/.

Nuccitelli, Dana. "Canada passed a carbon tax that will give most Canadians more money." *The Guardian, U.S. Edition*, October 26, 2018. https://www.theguardian.com/environment/climate-consensus-97-per-cent/2018/oct/26/canada-passed-a-carbon-tax-that-will-give-most-canadians-more-money.

"A Rabbinic Letter on the Climate Crisis." The Shalom Center. https://theshalomcenter.org/civicrm/petition/sign?sid=17.

Rattner, Steven. "Yes, We Need a Green New Deal. Just Not the One Alexandria Ocasio-Cortez Is Offering. There is a better way to reduce harmful emissions." *New York Times*, March 20, 2019. https://www.nytimes.com/2019/03/20/opinion/green-new-deal-carbon-taxes.html.

Reisner, Rabbi Avram Israel. *Al Pi Din*. January 2008.

Religious Action Center of Reform Judaism. "Position of the Reform Movement on the Environment." https://rac.org/position-reform-movement-environment.

Tamari, Meir. *With All Your Possessions: Jewish Ethics and Economic Life*. Northvale, N.J.: Jason Aronson Inc., 1987.

*Tanakh The Holy Scriptures. The New JPS Translation according to the Traditional Jewish Text*. Philadelphia: The Jewish Publication Society, 1985

United States Environmental Protection Agency. "Pulp and Paper Production (MACT I & III): National Emissions Standards for Hazardous Air Pollutants (NESHAP) for Source Categories." https://www.epa.gov/stationary-sources-air-pollution/pulp-and-paper-production-mact-i-iii-national-emissions-standards.

Waskow, Arthur. "Earth, Social Justice and Social Transformation: The Spirals of Sabbatical Release." In Waskow, *Torah of the Earth.*
The White House, Office of the Press Secretary. "Obama Administration Finalizes Historic 54.5 MPG Fuel Efficiency Standards." August 28, 2012. https://obamawhitehouse.archives.gov/the-press-office/2012/08/28/obama-administration-finalizes-historic-545-mpg-fuel-efficiency-standard.
White, Lynn, Jr. "The Historical Roots of Our Ecologic Crisis." *Science, New Series*, Vol. 155, No. 3767 (Mar. 10, 1967), pp. 1203–1207.

CHAPTER 6

# Usury

**Abstract** This chapter begins with a brief analysis of the determination of interest rates, followed by a discussion of usury from a historical perspective. An analysis of the Jewish teaching on usury—no interest is permitted on loans between Jews—follows, along with the problems this poses and the solutions the rabbis developed. This chapter concludes with an evaluation of payday loans, loans for small amounts of money for a short period of time: should they be prohibited, should there be a ceiling on the interest rate that is charged, are people better off with or without them?

**Keywords** Payday loans • Usury • Interest rates

## Introduction

*If you lend money to my people, to the poor among you, do not act toward them as a creditor; exact no interest from them.* (Exodus 22:24)

*Neither a borrower nor a lender be.* (*Hamlet*, Act I, Scene 3)

How could the U.S. economy function at all without interest-bearing loans? Few people in the United States could imagine life without borrowing money, with the expectation of paying interest. Most people use credit cards; most homeowners have a mortgage; most college students take out loans; and many people borrow to purchase a car.



N. R. Fox, *Profits and Prophets*,
https://doi.org/10.1007/978-3-030-40556-4_6

> Today, American society not only accepts credit as a way of life, we embrace it. The average American has $15,000 in credit card debt, $33,000 in student loan debt, and $156,000 in mortgage debt. Not only do the majority of the American public borrow their way up the income ladder, but federal mortgage and student loan markets and loose credit policies led to the creation of the American middle class. (Baradaran, p. 110)

The first section of this chapter will be a brief economic analysis of the rationale for charging interest on loans. Next section will be a review of Jewish social teaching on lending, including "*hetter iska*" and Hebrew Free Loan Societies (HFLSs). The last section will be an analysis of payday loans.

## Economic Analysis

*The cheap money which cannot be obtained is of little usefulness.* (Bowsher, p. 23)

Historically, interest was not charged for borrowing money. Either people considered money not productive—"barren"—so it made no sense for money to have a price (Hamilton), or lending at interest was considered "evil," so it was morally wrong to charge interest.

This attitude was strengthened in the Middle Ages by the Christians, whose attitude was "that money was evil … that to make money out of money by charging interest on a loan was the sin of usury" (Tuchman, p. 37). This was similar to biblical teachings that prohibited charging any interest at all (see Jewish Teaching on Usury and Interest). To get around the dilemma of needing to charge interest but being prohibited from doing so, "for practical purposes, usury was considered to be not the charging of interest per se but charging at a higher rate than was decent" (Tuchman, p. 38). Ultimately, that became the usual understanding of usury.

But in fact, money is productive, and it makes sense for money to have a price, a charge/fee for its use. In particular, there should be a price for a loan because the lender incurs a cost in so doing. Generally, economists consider three parts to that cost. First is the opportunity cost, which is the option lost by making the loan. For example, if I lend you $1000, I can no longer put that in a savings or a money market fund, where I would earn interest. In order for me to break even on the loan to you, at the very least I should be compensated by the amount I could have earned if I had kept that money. I should charge interest that would pay me whatever I would have earned had I put that $1000 in savings.

A second component of the cost of lending is inflation. If I lend you $1000, and you pay me back $1000 in a year after an inflation rate of 10%, then you are paying me back with "cheaper" dollars; in effect, I would have lost $100 because of the decrease in purchasing power over the year. Lastly, loans are risky (especially unsecured ones). Risk is harder to calculate than the other cost factors. There is always a chance that the loan will not be repaid, something that should be incorporated into the price of the loan to account for the possibility. If there is no interest charged on a loan, then the lender is actually subsidizing the borrower.

The critical question is what interest rate is low enough that people can afford it and high enough that banks (or other institutions) would be willing to make the loan. The *theoretical* economic analysis of anti-usury laws, which impose price ceilings, is similar to the effect of anti-price gouging and rent control laws.[1] They lower price below the market equilibrium level; suppliers will offer fewer loans, and consumers will demand more loans than they would at the market equilibrium price. Controls on interest rates benefit anyone who can obtain a loan at a lower interest rate and hurt anyone who was willing to pay a higher interest rate but cannot obtain a loan because the usury regulations have driven suppliers away. Is that person better off with no loans at a lower interest rate?

As is true in any completive market, the price serves a rationing function (Bowsher, p. 18), directing the product to consumers who value it and, at the same time, reflecting the cost of supplying them. Interest is the price of money. In a competitive market, price is determined by supply and demand. It does not reflect fairness, nor does it consider whether someone deserves the good or service at a certain price. It reflects efficiency. Interference with the market, even if it is well-intended, distorts incentives and sends inaccurate messages about cost and value. This is the principal, *conceptual*, reason that economists oppose restrictions on interest rates.

One of the first arguments against anti-usury laws came from Jeremy Bentham in 1787. He wrote "that no man of ripe years and of sound mind, acting freely, and with his eyes open, ought to be hindered, with a view to his advantage, from making such bargain, in the way of obtaining money, as he thinks fit: nor, (what is a necessary consequence) anybody hindered from supplying him, upon any terms he thinks proper to accede to" (Bentham). A contemporary editor to the letter adds that Bentham emphasized "the ability of individuals to be the best judges of their own particular circumstances, and their right to use their own best methods for the pursuit of happiness" (Bentham). In a more recent essay, Milton Friedman wrote, "I know of no economist of any standing from that time to this who has favored a legal limit on the rate of interest that borrowers could pay or lenders receive—though there must have been some. I know of no country that does limit by law the rates of interest—and I doubt there are any" (Friedman).[2]

In a study of the effects of the imposition of a rate ceiling in Washington, Roger Miller found that those who were most at risk financially were most likely *not* to be approved for loans. "[T]he people with the weakest credit worthiness, like welfare mothers, students, the elderly, and people with records of unstable employment, who were denied credit. On the other hand, those with the most wealth, the best jobs, and the highest probability of repaying the loans, were the ones who benefited from the reduced rate" (Bowsher, p. 18).

It is not surprising that bankers oppose price restrictions on interest rates. What might be surprising is the rationale that one banker presents. "Lenders have argued that keeping interest rates low, if it dries up all loans, is no favor to the consumer. Usury ceilings are not protection for consumers," said Bosies (Bill Bosies of the American Bankers Association). "When rates are at ceilings, what tends to happen is that loans dry up, and consumers don't get the money" (Hamilton). While it is somewhat disingenuous to cite bankers' views to support pro-consumer policies, in the case of the probable effects of limiting the level of interest rates, Mr. Bosies is most likely correct (even if bankers are also hurt by such limits).

Some have offered economic arguments in defense of anti-usury laws. Though the analysis may be valid, the policy prescription is not. Markets function efficiently under certain assumptions. Among them is that the parties have equal access to accurate information and that there is not disproportionate market power. Some have argued that borrowers, especially those without access to conventional sources, may be "concerned only with obtaining credit and do not even know what rate of interest they are paying" (Bowsher, p. 17). There is rarely evidence offered for this assertion, which appears to be based on the (assumed) demographic characteristics of the borrowers. See page 99 for data about the demographics of payday borrowers. And while it may have been more likely decades ago, today it is much easier for anyone to obtain information. Similarly, those supporting anti-usury laws argue that lenders have market power that enables them to control the market to the detriment of consumers. If true, either (or both) of these situations constitutes market failure, a situation where markets do *not* function efficiently and call for some sort of government intervention.

Even if one accepts the market failure argument, imposing a ceiling on interest rates is not the best solution. If consumers are uninformed and naïve, then instead of distorting the market, it makes more sense to provide resources to educate and assist these consumers. If banks and other sources of loans have disproportionate market power that enables them to "take advantage" of consumers, then take steps to curb that market power through antitrust laws or regulatory power over the lending institutions. Lowering interest rates does not address either of these sources of market failure directly and creates unnecessary inefficiencies.

## Jewish Teaching on Usury and Lending

> *You shall not deduct interest from loans to your countrymen, whether in money or food or anything else that can be deducted as interest; but you may deduct interest from loans to foreigners. Do not deduct interest from loans to your countrymen, so that the Lord your God may bless you in all your undertakings in the land that you are about to enter and possess.* (Deuteronomy 23:20–21)

Banks that charge interest are not usually condemned for doing so, and people who borrow for a home, a college education, or a car are not considered irresponsible. These types of exchanges could not be imagined in biblical times, when charging interest was prohibited.

The biblical prohibition against usury is more complex than it might seem at first. In contemporary times, "usury" is understood to mean charging interest at exorbitant rates. In the biblical texts, charging any interest *at all* is prohibited; there is no distinction made between a "reasonable and fair" interest rate and one that is exorbitant. Further, the biblical prohibition against charging interest applied only to loans between Jews. Charging interest to non-Jews was permitted. Understanding the rationale for the former informs the logic of the latter. What is not clear, however, is how any of this does apply or should be applied today.

Both biblical passages and Talmudic commentary permit Jews to charge interest to non-Jews, which allow us to draw two conclusions. Charging interest was not deemed to be immoral or unjust conceptually. If there were something immoral about charging interest, then no one should or would be charged. "Money may be borrowed from gentiles on usury and lent to them on usury, and the same applies with a resident alien" (*Baba Metzia*, 5:6). This suggests that the "Rabbis recognized that there was a sound economic base for interest charges ..." (Gordon, p. 118). While Jews were bound to the 613 commandments of the Bible, according to Jewish teaching, non-Jews were bound only to 7 commandments in the Noahide Covenant; all 7 refer to acts of immorality (murder, theft, adultery, etc.).[3] Usury is not among the prohibitions.

"This exemption could not have been granted if usury was considered a form of robbery or a violation of some other aspect of justice" (Kirschenbaum, p. 281). Why, then, would there be a distinction between laws that apply to Jews and non-Jews?

"This positive commandment to lend money to a fellow Jew is one of the examples in Judaism of *chesed*, an act of loving kindness" (Tamari, p. 170). Charging interest to a fellow Jew was an "undermining of the familial relationship" (Feldman, p. 241). "This explains why even reasonable rates of interest are forbidden. In a general context, they would not be predatory or immoral, but they are out of place among close family members" (Feldman, p. 242). Usury is one of the sins recited in the *Al Het* prayer on Yom Kippur. "And we have sinned against You by usury and extortion" (Greenberg and Levin, p. 519). There are even proscribed behaviors after the loan is made to preserve the borrower's human dignity. "It is forbidden for a man to appear before, or even to pass by, his debtor at a time when he knows that the latter cannot pay. He may frighten him or shame him, even if he does not ask for repayment" (Baron, p. 198).

As the prophet Ezekiel writes, charging interest is as severe an infraction as adultery and theft.

> [I]f a man is righteous and does what is just and right ... If he has not defiled another man's wife ... If he has not wronged anyone; if he has returned the debtor's pledge to him and has taking nothing by robbery; if he has given bread to the hungry and clothed the naked; *if he has not lent at advance interest or exacted accrued interest* ... If he has followed My laws and kept My rules and acted honestly—*he is righteous. Such a man shall live*—declares the Lord God ... (If he) has defiled another man's wife, has wronged the poor and the needy, has taken by robbery, has not returned a pledge ... has committed an abomination ... *(if he) has lent at advance interest or exacted accrued interest—shall he live? He shall not live!* If he has committed any of these abominations, he shall die; he has forfeited his life. (Ezekiel 18: 5–9, 13, emphasis mine)

The prophet Nehemiah recounts a time when Jews did charge one another interest, an act of desperation, when faced with a dire economic situation. This behavior outraged him. His demands of the people and their response are recounted in Baradaran, who notes the significance of the people acknowledging that they were behaving unfairly (p. 4).

> When I heard their outcry and these charges, I was very angry. I pondered them in my mind and then accused the nobles and officials. I told them, 'You are charging your own people interest!' ... 'You are selling your own people ... What you are doing is not right ... let us stop charging interest! Give back to them immediately their fields, vineyards, olive groves and houses, and also the interest you are charging them—one percent of the money, grain, new wine and olive oil.' 'We will give it back,' they said. 'And we will not demand anything more from them. We will do as you say.' (Nehemiah 5:1–13)

Does this mean that people were subsidizing family members by not charging interest? There was no stock market, no interest-bearing securities, so they did not lose money that way. The loss of liquidity was not viewed as a valid reason to charge interest to fellow Jews. Rabban Gamliel is cited as rejecting the view that loss of liquidity itself represents a cost which warrants a legitimate return by way of interest (*Baba Metzia* 5:10) (Gordon, p. 118).

Why is there no distinction between needy and prosperous Jews? In biblical times, the economy was predominantly agrarian. Loans were primarily personal, not for investment, but to provide for one's family. "A farmer's crop failed and as a result he was force to resort to a loan in order to purchase seed for planting the next year's crop. A person became temporarily incapacitated and was reduced to seeking a loan to put bread on the table" (Bleich, pp. 200–201). The reason someone needed a loan was to survive, not to enrich himself. In this context, a prosperous person would never need a loan.

Why a loan? Why not an outright gift? Jewish law is absolutely clear about its preference for loans over almsgiving. According to the Talmud, "He who lends [money] is greater than he who performs charity and he who puts in capital for partnership is greater than all" (*Sabbath 63a*) (Tenenbaum, p. 31). A loan is a greater act of *chesed*, loving kindness, than a gift, "for many people are humiliated at the thought of accepting a gift but not at accepting a loan" (Kirschenbaum, p. 289). Maimonides ruled that the interest-free loan is the highest form of charity, being an expression of the biblical commandment "Thou shalt give him [the needy] support" (Leviticus 25:35) (Tamari, p. 170).[4]

Over the centuries, Jews moved from living in a mostly agrarian society to one with more commerce. As Jews moved into cities in medieval times and were forbidden to own land, they turned to business, often becoming merchants. This created a dilemma, as the proscription of charging interest between Jews applied equally to personal and business loans. Without interest, who would offer a business loan? After all, a loan for business is not an act of *chesed*, loving kindness.

A distinction had to be made between loans whose purpose was to help the needy and loans for business. The rabbis created a work around, *hetter iska*, that preserves the law against charging interest and yet recognizes the need to charge interest for commercial needs (Kirschenbaum, p. 285, Bleich, pp. 197–198).

*Hetter iska* is a legal device by which a partnership is created between the borrower and the creditor. Its legal purpose is "to facilitate the lending of capital for commercial purposes [without violating the prohibition against charging interest]" (Bleich, p. 206). It does so by creating "a partnership arrangement as distinct from a debtor-creditor relationship" (Bleich, p. 198).[5] *Hetter iska* allowed Jews to charge and collect interest from fellow Jews without violating the law.

Hebrew Free Loan Societies (HFLS) began in the nineteenth century when Jewish immigrants came to the United States in large numbers. They offered interest-free loans for a variety of purposes. They filled a particular need among small businesses, most of which had no access to commercial loans (Tenenbaum, Chap. 2).[6] There were numerous reports of loan sharking, or similar practices, at the beginning of the twentieth century. *The New York Evening Post* published a story about a clerk, who earned $2400 annually, who borrowed $400. Four years later, he had paid back more than $2000 and still owed $1700 (Tenenbaum, p. 44).

Once commercial banks started making loans to small businesses and no longer made distinctions on the basis of religion, these free loan societies moved toward making personal loans to people in need.[7] Though begun as organizations exclusively for Jews, they have expanded to include persons of all (or no) faiths, where the loan is based purely on need.[8] There are literally no fees and no interest charged.

Remarkably, the Hebrew Free Loan Society in New York boasts a 99% repayment rate. The application process includes having a guarantor (which of course helps achieve that rate). The loan can be used for a variety of purposes including education and vocational training, housing, health care, addiction recovery, and general expenses.[9]

During the January 2019 partial government shutdown, the Philadelphia Hebrew Free Loan Society received an anonymous donation of $500,000 that enabled it to make loans of $1250 to government workers who were not being paid. The loans were available to any affected government worker, regardless of religious affiliation, whose salary was under $65,000. No interest was charged, no cosigners were required. The loan was to be repaid within 90 days after receiving the first paycheck after the shutdown was over (Orso).

## Payday Lending

*Basically, payday loans are the Lays potato chips of finance. You can't have just one, and they're terrible for you.* (John Oliver, "Last Week Tonight," August 11, 2014)[10]

*You don't need to be a math genius to know that it's a pretty bad deal if you're borrowing $500 and you have to pay back $1,000 in interest.* (President Obama, 2015)[11]

*Survey results show that almost 90 percent of (payday loan) users say that they're either somewhat satisfied or very satisfied with the product afterwards.* (Professor Robert DeYoung, University of Kansas)[12]

The biblical ideal of lending money without any interest has an important application to borrowing in the United States today. "It appears to address the widely condemned practice of usury, also known as predatory lending, where a lender exploits a borrower's desperate need for assistance by lending at rates of interest that are excessive and often unfeasible" (Feldman, p. 239). This could be the definition of payday loans.

### *What Is a Payday Loan?*

Payday loans are for small amounts of money for a short term. Customers are not typically destitute but rather low and middle income (LMI) (Caskey 2012, p. 682). The borrower needs to provide proof of a job and to have a bank account. People who are unemployed and/or "unbanked" are not eligible. Unlike more traditional loans, little additional information is required. Advance America, a major payday lender, requires the following for an application for a payday loan in person: government issued ID, proof of income, personal check, Social Security Number, and a checking account.[13]

### *Demographics of Payday Loan Customers*

The "picture" of a typical payday loan customer depends on what lens is being used. They frequently have a worse credit history and are more likely to have a history of bankruptcy than the average American and therefore have fewer options for alternative sources of funds (Stegman 2007, p. 173, Pew, pp. 8–10).

"It is a common misperception that payday borrowers are un-banked, in fact it is the exact opposite, only those with bank accounts can get a payday loan. Beyond having bank accounts, approximately one-third of payday borrowers are homeowners and more than half have graduated or attended college" (Klein).

Advance America describes its customers as middle income, educated, and working.[14] They claim that the average customer has a higher income (about $55,000 vs. $50,000), is better educated (78% with a high school diploma vs. 65%), and is more likely to own their own home (94% vs. 85%) than the average of the general population.[15] Stegman reports comparable numbers (Stegman 2007, p. 173).

Some characterize payday loan customers as unsophisticated, uninformed, and desperate (McLean). But others report that taking a payday loan is a deliberate and informed decision, the best choice among options. There is no credit check, a quick decision, and almost instantaneous access to the cash (Blair, p 6, Caskey 2005, p. 20). One study even found the customers are aware of the finance charge (Caskey 2012, p. 685). Customers also like the short term of the loan (Caskey 2012, p. 685). Given the data (see page 98) about the number of customers who are unable to repay the loan within the original two-week term, this is likely to be the main area of payday loans in which the customers are probably not making a truly informed choice.

## Economics of Payday Loans

Several questions must be answered in order to determine whether the payday loan industry requires oversight or not. All participants in a market must be making free and informed decisions in order for the outcome to be considered efficient. If that is not the case, as some claim regarding payday loan customers, then most economists would advocate for some sort of government intervention. On the other hand, if payday loans are restricted or even outright banned, as is the case in several states, are the people who would have taken out the loans better off? The answer depends, in part, on the alternatives they have. Most turn to payday loans for lack of better options—they have no credit card or are maxed out; they do not have sufficient funds in a checking account and so would have to pay an NSF (non-sufficient funds) fee. Of course, the last resort is to forego whatever they were going to use the funds for (see Stegman, p. 170).

The cost structure of the payday loan industry explains, in part, the high rates that are charged. With little to no information about the customer's ability to repay the loan (by design), the risk of default is higher than for more conventional loans. Underwriting a small, short-term loan is not profitable (McClean). One study found that defaults were 20% of operating expenses for payday lenders and only 3% for more conventional loans (McClean). Because a payday loan is so much smaller than a conventional loan, fixed costs are higher relative to total costs than in conventional loans (Caskey 2005, p. 20).

Many sources suggest that traditional banks are reluctant to enter the payday loan market for several reasons. They have concerns about their reputations, and they can make more money by charging fees on overdrafts and credits cards (Blair).

For reasons that are still not clearly understood, the economic model that predicts that prices will fall as competition increases does not apply to the payday loan industry. "[T]here is little evidence that a proliferation of payday lenders produces this consumer-friendly competitive effect. Quite the contrary: While states with no interest-rate limits do have more competition—there are more stores—borrowers in those states ... pay the highest prices in the country, more than double those paid by residents of some other states" (Maclean). Another study found that payday lenders charge the maximum permitted, indicating there is no price competition among firms (Blair). This could be explained in two different ways. Either the market is efficient, and the price is high because it has to cover costs in order for the firms to make a profit, or customers are so desperate they are insensitive to price increases (Blair). The industry claims it operates on a slim profit margin (Maclean) and that caps on interest rates and other regulations will put them out of business. Many states have either prohibited payday lenders or imposed caps so low that the companies cannot survive (Del Rio and Morrison).[16]

## Reality of Payday Loans

If most people actually paid off their loans in two weeks, there probably would not be so much controversy about them (Caskey 2012, p. 384). But numerous studies find this is not the case. While the loan is designed to be short term, often the borrower is unable to repay the loan on time, necessitating a second or even third or more loans. A 2012 Pew Report finds that "*on average, a borrower takes out eight loans of $375 each per year and spends $520 on interest.* … The average borrower is indebted about five months of the year" (emphasis mine).[17]

Given that the stated payday loan period is two weeks, is the annual percentage rate (APR) a relevant number to consider? Data from Pew[18] and the Consumer Financial Protection Bureau (CFPB)[19] suggest that there are enough payday customers who roll over their loans that, at the very least, the stated two-week interest rate is not the one that should be considered.

***Another misconception is that consumers use payday loans for unexpected emergencies. Here again the data indicate otherwise. "Most borrowers use payday loans to cover ordinary living expenses over the course of months,*** **not unexpected emergencies over the course of weeks"** (emphasis mine).[20]

A 2007 survey in California found that "50.2 percent said that they mainly used it (payday loans) to buy groceries or other household goods" (Caskey 2012, p. 684).

But the immediate need that consumers cite for needing a payday loan is really irrelevant—money is money. If someone needs to borrow money for a new car battery, that means they don't have enough steady income to support themselves. As Caskey writes, "If, for example, someone incurs an unexpected medical expense and then doesn't have enough money to buy groceries and takes out a loan, is the loan for the groceries or the medical expense?" (Caskey 2012, p. 684). A recent report from the Federal

Reserve found that "four in 10 adults, if faced with an unexpected expense of $400, would either not be able to cover it or would cover it by selling something or borrowing money" (Smialek).

The Pew Report indicates that without adequate cash for an expense and without a payday loan, "81 percent of borrowers say they would cut back on expenses. Many also would delay paying some bills, rely on friends and family, or sell personal possessions."[21]

## A Brief History of Lending

In the early 1900s, before credit was easily available to consumers, an illegal version of what we today call payday lenders emerged. Interest rates were exorbitant. In response, the Uniform Small Loan Law was passed in 1916. Among other things, it put a 3.5% cap on small loans (Pew 2012). Many states followed suit.

Consumer loans became more accessible in the mid-twentieth century. Deregulation and court decisions allowed banks to disregard state laws legally.[22] In the 1980s, many states eliminated or raised the caps on interest rates significantly (Baradaran, p. 109). At about the same time, banks stopped making small, unsecured loans because they could earn more by charging fees. Customers turned to payday lenders, where their credit history did not matter (Stegman, p. 171).

The number of payday lenders increased dramatically in the 1990s. As of 2008, there were more payday lenders in the United States than Starbucks and McDonald's combined (McLean). Today, there are about 14,300 payday loan storefronts in the United States (Cowley).

### *Regulations*

Many states have set a cap of 36% for the APR for payday loans.[23] But more than half of the states have much less restrictive regulations. In those states, the APR on a "typical" $300 payday loan ranges from 154% (Oregon) to 677% (Ohio).[24] In February 2019, Ohio's governor signed a new law that went into effect in October (2019), that caps the state's APR for payday loans at 60% (Hancock). References to payday loans have appeared in popular culture. In *Hope Never Dies: An Obama Biden Mystery*, Vice-President Biden makes the following reference to them when he describes a rundown Wilmington Delaware neighborhood: "These days, pawn stores were being replaced by check-cashing joints and payday-loan emporiums that had no qualms about taking advantage of the struggling American consumer during times of hardship" (Shaffer, p. 202).

In October 2017, after several years of study, the Consumer Financial Protection Bureau (CFPB) issued new regulations concerning payday loans that required lenders to determine whether the customer could repay the loan without extending it. "Lenders are required to determine whether the borrower can pay the loan payments and still meet basic living expenses and major financial obligations both during the loan and for 30 days after the highest payment on the loan."[25] Making a loan without such consideration is considered an "unfair business practice."[26]

Richard Cordray, the then-CFPB director, hailed the new regulations as "(bringing) needed reform to a market where far too often lenders have succeeded by setting up borrowers to fail," during a call with reporters to discuss the rule (Cowley). Not surprisingly, the industry saw things differently.

The new restrictions "will create credit deserts for many Americans who do not have access to traditional banking," said Edward D'Alessio, the executive director of Financial Service Centers of America, an industry trade group. Mr. D'Alessio said his group was "exploring every possible avenue" to abolish the rules (Cowley).

In February 2019, the new director of the CFPB proposed eliminating practically all of the requirements, stating that there was "insufficient evidence and legal support" for the provision (Cowley). A few days after that announcement, *The New York Times* published an editorial with the headline "Trump's Payback for Payday Lenders—The new head of the Consumer Financial Protection Bureau is seeking to gut rules that protect Americans from a predatory measure" (*The New York Times*, February 12, 2019).

## Payday Loans and the Military

There was much evidence that active military personnel took out payday loans much more frequently than the general population.[27] Explanations include their youth, regular paycheck, and highly concentrated residences on military bases (Tanik, p. 2). As a result, the Military Lending Act (MLA) was passed in 2006. Among other provisions, it set a 36% (APR) maximum rate on payday loans to all military personnel (Federal Register, p. 50580). Service members ranked financial concerns as even more stressful than deployments (Federal Register, p. 50580). Congress was motivated in part by the impact of such debt on military readiness (Federal

Register, p. 50581), especially while deployed overseas (Pascual). In August 2018, the Trump administration proposed relaxing some of the oversight of payday lenders to the military that the MLA required (Thrush).

## Conclusion

Our modern economy could not function without interest-bearing loans. There is a clear understanding that there is a cost to making a loan and that it is unreasonable to expect that a lender would make a loan without charging interest to the borrower. Institutions that make these loans are not regarded with contempt but rather as providing opportunities to advance economically, for example, by purchasing a home or going to college. Jewish tradition is perfectly clear—an interest-free loan is the best way to help some in need. The distinction between Jews and non-Jews is certainly not appropriate (and not even legal) today. There are numerous instances of Hebrew Free Loan Societies helping people of all or no faiths.

Are people better off with or without payday loans, what Caskey (2012) calls "the big question"? Some research (see especially Blair) indicates that banks and credit unions would be a better way to offer payday loans, but there are many reasons that is unlikely to happen.[28]

But there is a "*bigger* question." Why are these the only options available? Though economic research is inconclusive regarding whether people are better off with or without payday loans, that analysis is within the context of current alternatives—take out a payday loan and pay exorbitant (and what does that mean anyway?) interest rates, work overtime, risk a late fee on a bill, or do without. But the analysis would be different, if, for example, the United States had universal health care. Then an unexpected medical expense would not have the same financial consequences as it might now. If there were mandatory paid family leave, then a birth or illness would not affect earnings. If the federal minimum wage were higher, then workers would have a higher income.[29] Any policy for payday loans should be considered in the context of broader, structural economic reform.

## Notes

1. See Chap. 1 for a more extensive analysis of price ceilings.
2. This is an excellent example of the disconnect between economists and politicians to explain why politicians do not follow advice from economists in making policy. See Blinder for a discussion.

3. For more details about the Noahide Covenant, go to https://www.bc.edu/content/dam/files/research_sites/cjl/texts/cjrelations/resources/sourcebook/Noahide_covenant.htm.
4. See also Julie Salamon for how Maimonides' eight degrees of charity relates to contemporary charitable giving.
5. For more detail about *hetter iska*, an example of what is called *ha'aramah*, see Bleich. Much of his explanation is quite technical.
6. https://www.myjewishlearning.com/article/modern-tzedakah/.
7. https://www.myjewishlearning.com/article/modern-tzedakah/.
8. https://hfls.org/impact/.
9. https://hfls.org/impact/.
10. https://www.youtube.com/watch?v=PDylgzybWAw.
11. Dubner, http://freakonomics.com/podcast/payday-loans/.
12. Dubner, http://freakonomics.com/podcast/payday-loans/.
13. https://www.advanceamerica.net/loans/details/payday-loan#overview.
14. https://www.advanceamerica.net/loans/details/payday-loan#overview.
15. https://www.advanceamerica.net/news/consumer-issues/advance-americas-customer-demographics.
16. See http://www.ncsl.org/research/financial-services-and-commerce/payday-lending-state-statutes.aspx for regulations by state.
17. http://www.pewtrusts.org/~/media/legacy/uploadedfiles/pcs_assets/2012/pewpaydaylendingreportpdf.pdf, p. 9
18. http://www.pewtrusts.org/~/media/legacy/uploadedfiles/pcs_assets/2012/pewpaydaylendingreportpdf.pdf.
19. https://files.consumerfinance.gov/f/documents/Rulemaking_Payday_Vehicle_Title_Certain_High-Cost_Installment_Loans.pdf.
20. http://www.pewtrusts.org/~/media/legacy/uploadedfiles/pcs_assets/2012/pewpaydaylendingreportpdf.pdf, emphasis mine, p. 12.
21. http://www.pewtrusts.org/~/media/legacy/uploadedfiles/pcs_assets/2012/pewpaydaylendingreportpdf.pdf), p. 16).
22. In a unanimous decision in the landmark case *Marquette National Bank of Minneapolis v First of Omaha service Corp. Et al.*, the Supreme Court decided that the higher of two interest rates could be applied when a customer lived in a different start from the state in which the credit card was issued (https://h2o.law.harvard.edu/cases/4590).
23. Center for Responsible Lending, https://www.responsiblelending.org/research-publication/map-us-payday-interest-rates.
24. https://www.cleveland.com/open/2018/07/gov_john_kaisch_signs_payday_l.html.
25. https://files.consumerfinance.gov/f/documents/201710_cfpb_fact-sheet_payday-loans.pdf.

26. https://s3.amazonaws.com/files.consumerfinance.gov/f/documents/201710_cfpb_final-rule_payday-loans-rule.pdf.
27. Tanik (p. 1) reports that military personnel are three times as likely as civilians to take out a payday loan. In the early 2000s, Pascual finds that 44% of active duty military took out a payday loan, compared with 10% of all consumers.
28. One of the main obstacles is the banks themselves, as they are skeptical of the success and have concerns about their reputations (see Blair, p. 10).
29. See Chap. 3 for a fuller discussion of raising the minimum wage.

## Bibliography


Baradaran, Mehrsa. *How the Other Half Banks*. Cambridge, MA: Harvard University Press, 2015.

Baron, Salo W. *Ancient and Medieval Jewish History: Essays*. New Brunswick, N.J.: Rutgers University Press, 1972.

Bentham, Jeremy. *Defence of Usury*, 1787. https://oll.libertyfund.org/titles/bentham-defence-of-usury.

Blair, Sheila. "Low-Cost Payday Loans: Opportunities and Obstacles." The Annie E. Casey Foundation. June 2005.

Bleich, J. David. "Hetter Iska, the Permissible Venture: A Device to Avoid the Prohibition Against Interest-Bearing Loans." in Aaron Levine (ed). *The Oxford Handbook of Judaism and Economics*. Oxford University Press, 2010, pp. 197–220.

Blinder, Alan S. *Advice and Dissent: Why America Suffers When Economics and Politics Collide*. Basic Books, 2018.

Bowsher, Norman N. "Usury Laws: Harmful When Effective." Federal Reserve Bank of St. Louis, August, 1974, pp. 16–24. https://files.stlouisfed.org/files/htdocs/publications/review/74/08/Usury_Aug1974.pdf.

Caskey John P. "Fringe Banking and the Rise of Payday Lending." in *Credit Markets for the Poor*, Patrick Bolton and Howard Rosenthal, editors. New York, NY: Russell Sage Foundation, 2005, pp. 17–45.

Caskey, John P. "Payday Lending: New Research and the Big Question." In *The Economics of Poverty*, Phillip N. Jefferson, editor. Oxford University Press, 2012, pp. 681–706.

Center for Responsible Lending. Map of U.S. Payday Interest Rates. February 14, 2019. https://www.responsiblelending.org/research-publication/map-us-payday-interest-rates.

CFPB (Consumer Financial Protection Bureau) Rule of Pay Day lending. https://s3.amazonaws.com/files.consumerfinance.gov/f/documents/201710_cfpb_final-rule_payday-loans-rule.pdf.

CFPB (Consumer Financial Protection Bureau) Rule of Payday, Vehicle Title, and Certain High-cost Installment Loans. https://www.consumerfinance.gov/policy-compliance/rulemaking/final-rules/payday-vehicle-title-and-certain-high-cost-installment-loans/.

CFPB October 5, 2017 CFPB finalizes rule to stop payday debt traps. https://files.consumerfinance.gov/f/documents/201710_cfpb_fact-sheet_payday-loans.pdf.

Cowley, Stacy. "Payday Lending Faces Tough New Restrictions by Consumer Agency." *New York Times*, 10/05/2017. https://www.nytimes.com/2017/10/05/business/payday-loans-cfpb.html.

Dubner, Stephen J. "Are Payday Loans Really as Evil as People Say? (Ep. 241)." *Freakonomics Radio*, April 6, 2016. http://freakonomics.com/podcast/payday-loans/.

Feldman, Daniel Z. "The Jewish Prohibition of Interest: Themes, Scopes, and Contemporary Applications." in Aaron Levine (ed). *The Oxford Handbook of Judaism and Economics*. Oxford University Press, 2010, pp. 239–254.

Friedman, Milton. "Defense of Usury." *Newsweek*, April 6, 1970.

Gordon, Barry. *Economic Analysis Before Adam Smith: Hesiod to Lessius*. London: The Macmillan Press, 1975.

Hamilton, Martha H. "Usury Isn't What It Used to Be." *Washington Post*. May 11, 1980. https://www.washingtonpost.com/archive/business/1980/05/11/usury-isnt-what-it-used-to-be/378a2c48-5d20-469f-aa84-b5aa67ffcafb/?noredirect=on&utm_term=.5294158a1fac.

Hancock, Laura. "Gov. John Kasich signs payday lending bill." Cleveland.com, July 30, 2018. https://www.cleveland.com/open/2018/07/gov_john_kaisch_signs_payday_l.html.

Kirschenbaum, Aaron. "Jewish and Christian Theories of Usury in the Middle Ages." *Jewish Quarterly Review*. LXXV, No. 3, January 1985, pp. 270–89. https://www.jstor.org/stable/1454076?seq=1#page_scan_tab_contents.

Klein, Aaron. "Understanding non-prime borrowers and the need to regulate small dollar and 'payday' loans." The Brookings Institution, May 19, 2016. https://www.brookings.edu/research/understanding-non-prime-borrowers-and-the-need-to-regulate-small-dollar-and-payday-loans/.

*Last Week Tonight*, August 11, 2014 https://www.youtube.com/watch?v=PDylgzybWAw.

McLean, Bethany. "Payday Lending: Will Anything Replace it." *The Atlantic*. May 2016 https://www.theatlantic.com/magazine/archive/2016/05/payday-lending/476403/; http://freakonomics.com/podcast/payday-loans/.

Orso, Anna. "A Helping Hand: Anonymous Donor gives $500K for the furloughed." *Philadelphia Inquirer*, January 21, 2019, p. B1. https://www.inquirer.com/news/federal-government-shutdown-hebrew-free-loan-society-20190118.html.

Pascual, Al. "Why are payday loans so popular with the military?" *American Banker*. July 11, 2018. https://www.americanbanker.com/opinion/why-are-payday-loans-so-popular-with-the-military.

Pew Charitable Trust. "A Short History of Payday Lending Law." July 18, 2012a. https://www.pewtrusts.org/en/research-and-analysis/articles/2012/07/a-short-history-of-payday-lending-law.

Pew Charitable Trust. *Payday Lending in America: Who Borrows, Where they Borrow and Why*. July 2012b. http://www.pewtrusts.org/~/media/legacy/uploadedfiles/pcs_assets/2012/pewpaydaylendingreportpdf.pdf.

Salamon, Julie. *Rambam's Ladder: A Meditation on Generosity and Why It Is Necessary to Give*. Workman Publishing Company, 2003.

Shaffer, Andrew. *Hope Never Dies: An Obama Biden Mystery*. Philadelphia, PA: Quirk Books, 2018.

Smialek, Jeanna. "Many Adults Would Struggle to Find $400, the Fed Finds." *New York Times*. May 23, 2019. https://www.nytimes.com/2019/05/23/business/economy/fed-400-dollar-survey.html.

Stegman, Michael A. "Payday Lending." *Journal of Economic Perspectives*. Volume 21, Winter 2007, pp. 169–190.

Tamari, Meir. *With All Your Possessions: Jewish Ethics and Economic Life*. Northvale, N.J.: Jason Aronson Inc., 1987.

Thrush, Glenn. "Mulvaney Looks to Weaken Oversight of Military Lending." *New York Times*, August 10, 2018. https://www.nytimes.com/2018/08/10/us/politics/mulvaney-military-lending.html.

Tuchman, Barbara A. *A Distant Mirror: The Calamitous 14th Century*. New York: Alfred A. Knopf, 1978.

CHAPTER 7

# Conclusion

**Abstract** This chapter brings the concepts together, highlighting the differences in approaches, and concludes that there is a place for both market economics and Jewish social justice. Rebecca Blank, Provost at the University of Wisconsin, writes, "I am an economist and a Christian. As an economist, I believe in markets … the key question is not 'should there be a market?' (and implies the answer is certainly yes) but 'what are the limits to markets as an organizing structure for economics life?'" (Blank, pp. 12–13). She concludes, "there are times when other-interest is more important than self-interest, when we as a society need to respond more effectively to the human pain caused by market outcomes, and when 'freedom to choose' must give way to other values" (Blank, p. 54).

**Keywords** Market economics • Jewish social values • Values

Market economics and Jewish social thought offer different ways to analyze contemporary public policy issues. Market economics places an emphasis on achieving efficiency, assuming that individuals respond to incentives. Wants, not needs, are satisfied in a market system. Only preferences that are backed by the income to pay for them count, leaving some people wealthy and others sleeping on the street. This system results, under certain conditions, in producing the most goods and services possible at minimum cost but an inequitable distribution of income.



N. R. Fox, *Profits and Prophets*,
https://doi.org/10.1007/978-3-030-40556-4_7

Jewish social teaching places an emphasis on *tikkun olam*, repairing the world, based on compassion, justice, and righteousness. Repeatedly, Jewish texts command the Jewish community to think of others, to act with *chesed*, loving kindness. Individuals are acknowledged as consumers and workers but also as human persons, as parents, spouses, and members of a community. Jewish social teaching recognizes the human tendency of what economists would call strong greed, the desire to obtain as much of desired goods and services, and understands how that results in production and drive. At the same time, and distinct from market economics, Jewish social thought recognizes another tendency, the desire to care about other people and making sure they have the necessities of life, even if it means giving up something you have earned.

Economists are aware of the market's shortcomings and offer numerous ways to address them. And perhaps more surprising, Jewish texts often include explicit understanding of basic economic principles. Not offering a loan as the sabbatical year approaches and putting a cap on profits for necessities are examples that have been discussed earlier. In this way, they provide guidance on how to determine the trade-off between efficiency and equity. Taking both approaches into account results in more robust recommendations than would result from a single view because of the complexity of these public policy issues.

Throughout this book, I have analyzed various contemporary public policy issues through both lenses. Though on the surface they may appear to be in conflict, for several issues, the Jewish teaching supports the market economics recommendation. For others, they do indeed point to very different policies. And perhaps it is no surprise that teachings on how to treat fellow human persons are timeless.

Although the theory of wage determination predicts that raising the minimum wage will result in fewer jobs, most recent economic research shows that that net effect of an increase in minimum wage will be positive—significantly more people will see an increase in income than will experience job loss. This is especially true in today's strong economy, with a historically low unemployment rate and private firms paying their lowest paid employees almost double the federal minimum wage. Jewish social teaching is consistent and insistent that employers treat workers fairly, making sure they are paid on time in a way that allows them to support a family.

Economic and Jewish teaching on immigration point to the same pro-immigration policy recommendations, albeit for different reasons. Economic studies find that immigration is good for the U.S. economy.

"[I]f annual United States immigration stayed at only 200,000 (its 2018 level, 70% less than the previous year) rather than a more normal one million, gross domestic product would be $1 trillion lower a decade from now" (Goolsbee). And because funding for Social Security and Medicare depends on contributions from current workers, more immigrants will support funding for those programs (Goolsbee).

At the microeconomic level, most studies show that immigrants have little to no negative impact on native wages and that lower cost immigrant labor can lower prices on final products and increase employment for workers with complementary skills.

The Jewish perspective could not be clearer—Jews are to care for the stranger, the *ger*, because they themselves were strangers in foreign lands. Strangers are considered to be vulnerable, just as widows and orphans are, and therefore need and deserve special care. Certainly, this is true for current immigrants to the United States.

Although Jewish texts explicitly recognize the economic concept that explains many environmental problems, the policy prescription is different from the economics solution.[1] Most economists support policies of taxation on actions that contribute to climate change to pay for the cost within a market context, as opposed to government fiat. Taxes would reduce emissions, though not to zero.

Jewish teaching privileges community over the individual in cases of environmental degradation. Behavior that creates pollution is prohibited. With some exceptions, financial compensation to the individuals who are harmed is not allowed. This is in direct contrast to the market remedy of a tax on such behavior. Health concerns are paramount. Concern for the environment is both for the present and for the future, because people are stewards of the earth, which belongs to God. "The earth is the Lord's and all that it holds, the world and its inhabitants" (Psalm 24.1).

Economists recognize that there are costs to making loans, so it is fair to charge a positive interest rate, at least enough to recoup those costs, and unreasonable to expect that someone would offer a loan interest free. Under ancient Jewish law, debts were to be forgiven during the sabbatical year, and Jews were forbidden to charge interest to fellow Jews but were permitted to charge interest to non-Jews. These rules would be difficult to implement today. But "the values behind the laws speak directly to the modern reality of rampant consumer debt, deceptive loan practices ..." (Brandow). These values can provide guidance when considering policy about payday loans.

Rebecca Blank writes, "I am an economist and a Christian. As an economist, I believe in markets" (Blank, p. 11).[2] "The key question is not 'Should there be a market?' but 'What are the limits to markets as an organizing structure for economic life?'" (Blank, pp. 12–13). She reminds us of several things that economists tend to overlook in their zeal to promote and defend the market. Among them is the importance of placing economic concerns alongside other values and needs (Blank, p. 5).

She concludes, "there are times when other-interest is more important than self-interest, when we as a society need to respond more effectively to the human pain caused by market outcomes, and when 'freedom to choose' must give way to other values" (Blank, p. 54).

Market economics and the Jewish social tradition have different purposes. As Alan Blinder once wrote, "the unfettered market system shows no mercy" (Blinder 1988, p. 27). The Jewish social tradition champions the need for "mediating the effects of the market economy" (Blank, pp. 5–6).

## Notes

1. Even though the texts do not use the economic term *externalities*.
2. Although Blank writes as an economist and a Christian, her questions and conclusions reflect Jewish values and could have been written by someone like me, an economist and a Jew.

## Bibliography

Blank, Rebecca. *Is the Market Moral? A Dialogue on Religion, Economics, and Justice* (with William McGurn). Washington, D.C.: Brookings Institution, 2004.

Blinder, Alan S. *Hard Heads, Soft Hearts: Tough-minded Economics for a Just Society*. New York: Basic Books, 1988.

Brandow, Jonathan. "There's Gleaning to Do: How Ancient Sabbatical Laws can work in a Modern Economy." *Tablet*, October 6, 2014. https://www.tabletmag.com/jewish-life-and-religion/185127/shmita-modern-economy.

Goolsbee, Austan. "Sharp Cuts in Immigration Threaten U.S. Economy." *New York Times*, October 11, 2019. https://www.nytimes.com/2019/10/11/business/immigration-cuts-economy.html.

# Index[1]



[1] Note: Page numbers followed by 'n' refer to notes.



N. R. Fox, *Profits and Prophets*,
https://doi.org/10.1007/978-3-030-40556-4

The manufacturer's authorised representative in the EU is Springer Nature Customer Service Centre GmbH, Europaplatz 3, 69115 Heidelberg, Germany. If you have any concerns regarding our products, please contact ProductSafety@springernature.com

Printed and bound by CPI Group (UK) Ltd, Croydon, CR0 4YY
30/09/2026
02225475-0009